People, Politics and Power

FROM O'CONNELL TO AHERN

Stephen Collins

THE O'BRIEN PRESS
DUBLIN

First published 2007 by The O'Brien Press Ltd
12 Terenure Road East, Rathgar, Dublin 6, Ireland.
Tel: +353 1 4923333; Fax: +353 1 4922777
E-mail: books@obrien.ie
Website: www.obrien.ie

ISBN: 978-0-86278-985-5

Typesetting, editing, layout, design © copyright
The O'Brien Press Ltd

British Library Cataloguing-in-Publication Data
Collins, Stephen, 1951-
People, politics and power : from O'Connell to Ahern
1. Ireland - Politics and government - 19th century
2. Ireland - Politics and government - 20th century
3. Ireland - History - 19th century 4. Ireland - History - 20th century
I. Title
941.5'08

1 2 3 4 5
07 08 09 10

Editing, typesetting and design: The O'Brien Press Ltd
Printing: Cox and Wyman Ltd

Photographs used with kind permission: George Munday; The Irish Image
Collection; *The Irish Times*; The Green Party; *Irish Independent*.

Acknowledgements

The idea for a short book on Irish political history was suggested to me by Michael O'Brien and Ide ní Laoghaire, and I would like to thank them both for their support as the project evolved. Special thanks to my editor at The O'Brien Press, Síne Quinn, whose pertinent observations, patience and editing skills helped the project along. To Emma Byrne for the cover design and Erika McGann for production.

I would like to thank a number of friends, particularly Barry Desmond, Ted Hallett, Maurice Manning and Joseph O'Malley for reading the draft, correcting mistakes and suggesting improvements. Any errors or omissions are my own responsibility.

Thanks is also due to the staff of the National Archives, the National Library and the Oireachtas Library for their courtesy and professionalism, and also to Irene Stevenson of *The Irish Times* for her help with the photographs.

Finally, I would like to thank my wife Jean for correcting the initial draft and making valuable suggestions as well as for her help and encouragement.

CONTENTS

INTRODUCTION

Politics in Ireland is something of a national obsession. Despite a decline in voter turnout in recent general elections, politics still attracts huge interest and a good political controversy has the capacity to get the whole country talking and arguing like nothing else. Powerful political figures like Charles Haughey, Eamon de Valera, Charles Stewart Parnell and Daniel O'Connell dominated Irish politics at different times over the past two centuries and defined their eras. The great election campaigns waged by these politicians, and the controversies in which they were involved, have left a deep imprint on all aspects of Irish life, from law to literature, from economics to family life.

The fondness of Irish people for politics turns election counts into something akin to great sporting events. A large swathe of the population tunes in to radio and television for the count, which normally takes two days under the single transferable vote system of proportional representation. The attempt by the Government to streamline the system and eliminate the lengthy counts through the introduction of nationwide electronic voting in 2004 ended in ignominy. This was partly because of concerns for the accuracy and security of the proposed voting machines but mainly because people were not willing to be cheated out of a great national event that happens only every few years. The democratic nature of Irish society and the fondness of its citizens for politics is hard to reconcile with the popular version of Irish history that focuses on a succession of rebellions against British rule, culminating in the 1916 Rising and Irish independence in 1922. The reality is that for at least a century before independence most Irish people, most of the time, engaged in the democratic process and found in it the means of expressing their aspirations, including their desire for national independence. Often it was not the national struggle but unvarnished local political issues that aroused the strongest passions in election campaigns.

Irish people themselves are often surprised to learn that the country is one of the oldest continuous democracies in Europe. The survival of Irish democracy since 1922 was facilitated by the country's geographical position, sheltered from invasion as an island on the western fringe of Europe between Britain and the United States. The reasons for its healthy democracy, though, go deeper than that. The involvement of Irish people in party politics in the century before independence enabled parliamentary democracy to put down such strong roots that it was able to survive revolution and civil war at home and the political chaos that overtook most of Europe in the 1930s and 1940s.

This book takes its starting point with the rise of Daniel O'Connell and the creation of a mass democratic movement that changed Ireland and influenced the wider world. Of course politics didn't just begin in the 1820s with Catholic Emancipation. The Irish parliamentary tradition goes back all the way to the Middle Ages. It evolved into the Irish Parliament of the eighteenth century which had many comparable features to the politics of today. Powerful politicians like Henry Grattan, Henry Flood and John Philpot Curran made a lasting impression on Irish life. There were close fought constituency elections and bitter struggles between individuals and factions for power and influence. However, the Parliament on College

Green in Dublin was a purely Protestant affair and its political disputes did not involve the Catholic majority. Although later generations of Irish nationalists looked back on this Parliament as being a significant milestone on the road to freedom, because it asserted a degree of independence from the British Parliament in 1782, it was never democratic in any real sense because the majority of the population was excluded.

It did bow a little to democracy in 1793 when Catholics were allowed to vote but they were still excluded from Parliament, the law and senior positions in state employment, including the Army. When rebellion swept across Leinster and parts of Ulster in 1798 the British Government decided that the only way the country could be governed effectively was to abolish its one-sided Parliament and bring the country directly under the control of Westminster. The Irish Parliament was persuaded to vote itself out of existence with promises of jobs and peerages providing an inducement and 100 Irish seats were added to the House of Commons.

The leaders of Catholic Ireland actually welcomed the Act of Union, believing there was a much better chance of fair treatment from the Parliament in London than from the Protestant ruling class at home. The Prime Minister, William Pitt, promised that Catholic Emancipation would follow on from the Union but he was prevented from delivering on his promise by the bitterly anti-Catholic King George III and he resigned from office in frustration. Pitt was just the first in a succession of leading British politicians to lose their jobs over Ireland. The freedom to participate fully in politics was denied to the leaders of Catholic Ireland for almost three decades after the Union. It was the failure to deliver emancipation that ultimately ensured the Union would come to be hated by the majority of Irish people.

Daniel O'Connell channelled opposition to the Union into political action in the 1820s in a political campaign that shaped the course of Irish politics for the rest of the nineteenth century and arguably down to the present day. As the franchise was widened during the nineteenth century, and more people allowed to vote, everyday bread and butter concerns often had as much impact on the political scene as great national issues. The tactics and political organisation developed by O'Connell were exported by Irish emigrants to Britain, the United States, Australia and other British colonies and in turn influenced the development of western parliamentary democracy.

For all that, politics takes a back seat in the popular version of Irish history which usually focuses on violence, revolution and British retribution. The Irish state itself regularly commemorates the violent actions of bygone days and virtually ignores great political figures and events from the past. The nintieth anniversary of the 1916 Rising was commemorated with great pomp and circumstance in 2006, while the execution of the Manchester Martyrs in 1867 was planned as the big commemorative event of 2007. By contrast the anniversaries of O'Connell, Parnell or the Land League founder, Michael Davitt, come and go with little attention from the state.

This is not to deny the importance of revolutionary violence as a significant element in shaping the course of Irish history. There is no arguing with the fact that the 1916 Rising jolted mainstream Irish nationalism on to a faster track towards independence. The problem is that, taken in isolation, the commemoration of violent acts distorts the past and provides an inadequate explanation for the present. This leads to multiple layers of contradiction and irony in a country whose 'official history' belies its true nature.

The modern Irish state is a smooth running parliamentary democracy committed to the rule of law and an enterprise economy. Irish sovereignty has been pooled through the European Union and relations with Britain are good, with the two governments working closely together to deal with the residual problems of Northern Ireland.

It is worth pondering which of the imposing figures of the past would find this state more congenial. The great political leaders from O'Connell to Redmond would surely feel at home in the Dáil chamber and be proud of the country's independence and economic success. The good working relationship between the governments of Ireland and Britain in the twenty-first century would be another source of gratification.

On the other hand it is hard to believe that leaders of the 1916 Rising who seized control of Irish nationalism from Redmond would be quite as happy. Modern Ireland is hardly the Gaelic speaking, anti-materialist country dreamed of by Padraig Pearse when he made his blood sacrifice. Neither is it the dictatorship of the proletariat envisaged by James Connolly.

For all that, it is equally ironic that the modern Irish democratic state was created by the heirs of Pearse and Connolly. The Sinn Féin movement that swept the Irish Parliamentary Party away in 1918 followed the tried and trusted rules of mass political agitation pioneered by the very politicians they despised. Despite violence and civil war, the

Sinn Féin leaders deliberately established a liberal parliamentary democracy. Later when Eamon de Valera, the most famous surviving commandant of 1916, failed in his attempt to challenge the Free State in arms he founded his own political party, Fianna Fáil. He then went on to dominate Irish life through political action and party organisation in a manner reminiscent of O'Connell and Parnell.

Fianna Fáil has always sought to portray itself as the expression of the spirit of 1916. While its republican associations are clearly an element of its appeal to the voters, the party has much deeper roots in the democratic Irish past, otherwise it could never have been so phenomenally successful. That success has been sustained over the decades by the hard graft of political activity that has made it the biggest party in every election since 1932.

It is certainly arguable that politics and elections have had a more profound influence on the way we are today than violence and insurrections. This book attempts to tell the story of modern Irish politics and to give the politicians, for all their widely perceived faults and failings, their due.

CHAPTER ONE

FROM THE LIBERATOR
TO THE CHIEF

Daniel O'Connell was the first great democratic political leader
to emerge in Ireland. In fact O'Connell's political genius was
such that he transformed British as well as Irish politics and had
an influence right across Europe. Born in 1775 to a wealthy
land-owning Catholic family in Kerry, O'Connell studied briefly
in France where he witnessed the early excesses of the French
Revolution. This experience had a profound influence over his
political thinking and his attitude to violent revolution as a
means of political change was reinforced by the horrors of the
1798 Rebellion.

O'Connell qualified as a barrister in London and made his
first foray into politics in 1800 when he was among the
minority of educated Catholics who opposed the Act of
Union. Over the following two decades he achieved fame as a
barrister and as a champion of the Catholic cause. Tall and
burly with inexhaustible energy, the prerequisite of a truly
successful politician, O'Connell had a booming voice and a
natural ability to dominate a courtroom or political meeting.
He could switch at ease from passion to buffoonery, from
intellectual argument to emotive appeal. In political debate he
used vituperation and humour in equal measure as he changed
tack according to the opportunities available to him. He spent
vast amounts of money – much of it raised for him by his
supporters – and had a reputatio probably false, as a
womaniser. Ironically, for one who rejected violence in favour

of political action, O'Connell achieved the status of a national hero by fighting a duel against a leading representative of Protestant opinion in Dublin. The row began when O'Connell ridiculed 'the beggarly Corporation of Dublin' in 1815 and was challenged to a duel by one of its leading members John D'Esterre. Feeling that he could not refuse the challenge, O'Connell agreed and, in the exchange of shots, fatally wounded his opponent. O'Connell, stricken with remorse, vowed never to fight again and settled a pension on D'Esterre's widow.

Whatever about his own feelings of guilt, the incident added to O'Connell's mythic stature among Irish Catholics, particularly the impoverished, uneducated masses. In 1823 O'Connell founded the Catholic Association with the objective of securing emancipation. Initially the Association attracted land-owning and middle-class Catholics into its ranks but O'Connell turned it into a national movement in 1824 through the introduction of the Catholic Rent which allowed poorer people to join for a penny a month. The involvement of the Catholic clergy in the organisation helped turn it into a crusade involving all classes of society, with branches in almost every parish in the country. Public meetings were held and newspapers launched in support of the campaign which widened out from the purely legal disabilities against Catholics into a range of issues affecting the majority of the population. The tithes, under which everybody, including Catholics, had to pay a sizeable annual tax for the support of the Established Church, was one of the most emotive of the issues affecting the mass of the people and it provoked widespread violence in the 1820s and 1830s.

The movement began to have a direct impact on politics in the general election of 1826 in which it supported a number of Protestant Liberal candidates. Matters were brought to a head with O'Connell's decision to stand in a by-election in County Clare in 1828. Before that Catholic voters had been encouraged to support Protestant candidates who favoured emancipation. O'Connell, by standing himself threw down the gauntlet to the state. Poorer Catholic voters, known as 'forty shilling freeholders', rallied to O'Connell's cause and defied their landlords who supported his rival Vesey-Fitzgerald. O'Connell won by 2057 votes to 982. The election of a Catholic, who was legally debarred from taking his seat in the House of Commons, provoked a political crisis in Britain.

The Prime Minister at the time was another Irishman but one of a very different stripe to O'Connell. Arthur Wellesley, the Duke of Wellington, and victor of Waterloo was one of the greatest military strategists of his own, or any other, age and a British national hero. Born in Dublin in 1769 of a powerfully connected Meath land-owning family, originally named Colley, Wellington had served as an MP for Trim in the Irish Parliament between 1790 and 1795. Contrary to myth he was not ashamed of his Irish birth and never uttered the phrase 'being born in a stable doesn't make you a horse', which is often falsely attributed to him. Wellington, though, was a Protestant Tory aristocrat and a fervent supporter of the Union. Still, as a shrewd leader of men he recognised that the election of O'Connell had transformed the political situation and threatened to lead to an explosion of violence in Ireland if emancipation was again denied. To the horror of his ultra-Tory supporters Wellington put through the Catholic Relief Act in

April 1829, lifting all the legal disabilities against Catholics. O'Connell had demonstrated that political activity backed by nationwide organisation could force the British Government to come to terms with Irish grievances.

O'Connell's victory influenced the wider movement for political reform across the UK. There was immediate pressure for a fundamental change in the electoral system, with its myriad of 'pocket boroughs', which was effectively in the hands of the landed proprietors. The result was the 1832 Reform Act, which marked the first decisive step towards fully democratic government accountable to Parliament. In Ireland O'Connell moved on from emancipation to develop a wider political programme based on the repeal of the Act of Union. He led an organised party into the general election of 1832 committed not only to Repeal but to a detailed programme of reform. It was the first time a political party anywhere in Europe contested an election by presenting the voters with a party programme. Repeal clubs and Liberal clubs sprang up all over the country, nationalist newspapers proliferated and people gathered in houses, shebeens and meeting halls to discuss the great issues of the day. The mood is captured in one of Padraic Column's most evocative poems:

Down here they have but tale and song,
They talk Repeal the whole night long.

Every candidate standing for O'Connell's party had to take a pledge to vote for repeal of the Act of Union if elected. They also committed themselves to support a range of policies aimed at reforming the Government of Ireland including abolition of the tithes, regular parliamentary elections, a fair jury system and police reform. More surprisingly pledges were also required from candidates to vote for the abolition of Negro slavery and the emancipation of the Jews. O'Connell has rightly gone down in history as a champion of the Catholic cause in Ireland but his world-view was not limited to the grievances of his own people. 'For the rights of Catholics and universal liberty,' was how he once summed up his political philosophy. Gladstone recalled how O'Connell had 'poured out his wit, his pathos and his earnestness in the cause of negro emancipation.'

O'Connell's party emerged as the largest in Ireland in 1832 winning 42 of the 105 Irish seats in the Commons as against 33 for the Liberals and 30 for the Conservatives. An inevitable response to O'Connell's victory on emancipation was that it provoked a counter reaction among Irish Protestants who banded together, despite their many differences, to support the Union. This sectarian element to politics was there from the very beginning and it has had direct consequences right down to the twenty-first century. An electoral map of the 1832 election shows the country divided along lines that predated partition by almost a century. All of Ulster returned Conservative MPs committed to the Union and the Protestant cause. Dublin, Leinster, Munster and Connacht split between the Repeal Party led by O'Connell and Liberals who supported emancipation but were less enthused by the idea of Repeal. A few stray Liberals were elected in Ulster, and a few Conservatives outside it, but the political map of Ireland that has persisted to this day is clear from that first genuine national election in 1832.

For the rest of the 1830s the country was gripped by a bitter political struggle between the increasingly assertive Catholic majority outside Ulster and the Protestant minority who fought a rearguard action to retain power throughout the island. A parliamentary inquiry into illegal voting practices in County Longford provides a unique insight into the politics of the period. There were two vital differences with politics of today. Only the better off were eligible to vote and voting was a public rather than a private affair. Traditionally that gave landlords power to pressurise tenants into supporting their preferred candidate. With the rise of O'Connell, though, even stronger pressure was applied from the opposite direction with the Catholic clergy and the unenfranchised masses providing an even more intimidating counter weight.

At election time in Longford the few hundred eligible Catholic voters from each parish, accompanied by thousands of non-voters, were led in formation into the county town to vote, with the parish priest riding at the head of each troop. Conservative voters, mainly Protestant, were led into town by their landlords in a similar fashion. Each side brought up groups of five men at a time to the polling station to publicly declare their allegiance. This process went on for days and the town was thronged with crowds in a state of high, and often drunken, excitement. The thousands of non-voters were plied with free drink by each side to 'encourage' the registered voters to do the right thing. The result did not begin to emerge until one side ran out of voters. When that happened the other side continued to bring their people into the polling stations for only as long as necessary to secure a majority and voting came to a rapid conclusion. In Longford Repealers and Conservatives had almost identical numbers registered to vote at a succession of elections. Voters were kidnapped, beaten and even killed during the 1830s as the two factions struggled for supremacy.

Although they could not vote many women took an interest in politics. The Longford inquiry was told that the wife of one tenant farmer refused to sleep with her husband unless he voted for the O'Connellite candidate, Luke White. Another Longford woman became famous all over Ireland for her intervention in a by-election in 1837. When Peter Prunty, a Catholic voter, was allegedly taken from his home under duress to vote for the Conservative Protestant candidate, Thomas Lefroy, his wife decided to take action. As Prunty and other freeholders were escorted into Longford town to vote for the Conservative candidate, his wife was among the thousands who thronged the streets. As he passed by she called out: 'Oh Prunty, remember your soul and your liberty.' With his wife's words ringing in his ears he entered the polling station and shouted out his vote for Luke White, despite his Tory escort. O'Connell wrote a public letter from Tralee congratulating Mrs Prunty and suggesting that the Catholic Association should 'testify their respectful admiration' of her conduct by presenting her with a shawl or other suitable article.

With a well-disciplined party behind him in the House of Commons, O'Connell became an important figure in British politics, initiating and supporting radical and reforming legislation. After the 1835 election his party held the balance of power and used that position to do a deal with the Liberal/Whig Government to force the Tories out of office. In what became known as the Lichfield House compact O'Connell and the Liberal leaders came to a tacit understanding that the Irish would support a Liberal

Government in exchange for measures of practical reform. It set the template for Irish nationalists for the rest of the nineteenth century and into the twentieth century. The objective was to achieve the balance of power in the Commons and use it to extract concessions from the British Government.

The Lichfield House compact worked reasonably well. Legislation on municipal reform further democratised Irish politics and enabled O'Connell himself to become the first Catholic Lord Mayor of Dublin since the 1680s. Reform of the tithes removed a serious source of dissention. The administration in Dublin became much more even handed, with middle-class Catholics and Liberal Protestants obtaining office in significant numbers for the first time. Policing became more balanced and the Orange Order was forced to dissolve for fear of suppression.

When the Liberals lost office in 1841 the deal died and O'Connell switched from pragmatic political manoeuvre back to radical agitation for the repeal of the Union. He addressed a series of 'monster meetings' around the country the most famous being at the Hill of Tara attended by hundreds of thousands of people. The Tory Government became alarmed at the growing strength of the movement, particularly at a plan to elect a Council of 300, which threatened to become the de facto Government of Ireland. O'Connell had arranged another 'monster meeting' at Clontarf in October 1843, which was planned as the climax of the campaign and vast crowds were on the way there when it was banned by the Government. Unwilling to risk bloodshed, O'Connell called off the meeting. He was arrested, charged with conspiracy and sentenced to a year in prison. The conviction was overturned by the House of

Lords after O'Connell had spent nearly six months in prison – but it marked a turning point. O'Connell was now nearly 70 and the experience sparked a physical decline as well as a more cautious approach to politics. That in turn provoked a split in the Repeal movement with the Young Ireland faction leaving to pursue the nationalist agenda by violent means, if necessary. When O'Connell died in Genoa in 1847, on his way to Rome, his country was being ravaged by the Great Famine.

While his campaign for Repeal failed, O'Connell's achievements were extraordinary. He earned the title of 'The Liberator' because he was a figure like Ghandi or Mandela who inspired his people with a sense of their own worth and gave them the courage to seek freedom and justice. Balzac said of O'Connell that he 'incarnated a whole people'. To the impoverished Catholic masses he was, in the words of Frank O'Connor, 'a hero personification of themselves.' In practical terms O'Connell politicised his people and taught them how to use parliamentary democracy in pursuit of reform and ultimately nationhood. He changed British politics by leading the first party to the Commons committed to a specific programme and he became a hero and a model to Catholic liberals across Europe by remaining a staunch member of his church while rejecting the right of the Vatican to command obedience on anything outside the strictly religious sphere.

After O'Connell's death Irish politics entered a quieter phase for the next 30 years. The 1848 rebellion by the Young Irelanders was a small-scale affair that caused fewer deaths than most election campaigns. During the 1850s and 1860s most Irish politicians described themselves as either Liberals or Conservatives and went along with their counterparts from

Scotland, England and Wales in the House of Commons. Some took Government office when it was offered. Irish MPs fitted into the broad categories of Liberal or Conservative as far as Commons business was concerned with most of those from nationalist Ireland describing themselves as Liberals.

A party led by James Sadlier and William Keogh committed to tenant rights emerged in the 1850s but it fizzled out when Sadlier committed suicide on Hampstead Heath and Keogh accepted office as Irish Attorney General.

The flavour of Irish politics at this period is captured by the Victorian writer, Anthony Trollope's series of great political novels, featuring Phineas Finn, a fictional MP from Killaloe in County Clare. As in Trollope's novel, campaigns for tenant rights occupied Irish farmers rather than the repeal and in many constituencies it came down purely to personality politics with candidates vying with each other in promises to the voters. Money was splashed about with abandon and drink bought in enormous quantities at election time to 'encourage' voters to do the right thing.

The franchise was widened in stages through the nineteenth century and a greater proportion of the population became eligible to vote. In 1873 the secret ballot was introduced and voters no longer had to declare their preference in public. This further reduced the influence of landlords over their tenants although in truth that practice had long passed. By the middle of the nineteenth century voters were much more likely to be influenced by the Catholic clergy than their landlords in their choice of politicians.

In the 1870s the national question returned as a serious political issue. The small Fenian rebellion in 1867 failed to capture popular imagination and did little to undermine the Union. However, agitation for the release of Fenian prisoners and an incident in Manchester inflamed public opinion in nationalist Ireland. Two leading Fenians were being transported from the courthouse in Manchester to jail when the prison van was attacked and the men freed. An unarmed policeman was shot dead during the incident and the authorities rounded up Fenian suspects. Three of them, Allen, Larkin and O'Brien, were convicted and hanged in November 1867. The Manchester Martyrs, as they became known, sparked a groundswell of popular support for the Fenians and provided the basis for launching the Home Rule movement. This was initially led by the conservative Isaac Butt. He envisaged Home Rule as providing for a devolved parliament in Ireland to run local affairs, with foreign policy and taxation being left with the central government in Westminster and the same sovereign being recognised by both countries.

A slate of 60 Home Rule candidates was elected to the Commons in 1874 – the biggest ever Irish party at Westminster. Many of the MPs were landlords and their opinions were varied. Some of them viewed Home Rule as a means of preserving the landed interest in a new political arrangement. However, as the decade wore on the growing prominence of former Fenians and the involvement of the Catholic clergy changed the character of the movement. The rise to prominence of a Protestant landlord from County Wicklow, Charles Stewart Parnell, marked the transformation to a much more radical form of politics.

A cold, aloof and even arrogant figure Parnell became a politician of note very rapidly after his election to the

Commons in 1875. He was soon the acknowledged leader of the more militant faction in the Home Rule party, through the adoption of obstructionist tactics in parliament. These tactics involved spinning out debates for days on end with incredibly long speeches and using every possible device to prevent parliament doing its business. The result was interminably long sessions that went on day and night and provoked changes in the rules of the Commons to enable the chamber to function. Queen Victoria was so concerned that she wrote to her Prime Minister, Disraeli, in 1880 asking: 'Ought you not to come to some arrangement with some of the sensible and reasonable and not violent men on the other side, to put a stop to what clearly is a determination to force the disruption of the British Empire.' Disraeli wrote back to say that 'there are no "sensible and really not violent men" in the ranks of the Opposition on whom your Majesty might now act.'

Parnell followed up obstruction with the 'new departure'. This involved a tacit alliance with the Fenians, and Parnell's acceptance of the presidency of the Land League, which was dedicated to the destruction of landlordism. The League was the creation of a former Fenian, Michael Davitt. Parnell's presidency of the organisation gave him such a prominent position that in 1880 he became chairman of the Irish Parliamentary Party in the Commons as the Home Rulers became known. For the next decade Parnell was the dominant political figure in Ireland and a major player in British politics. The Land Act of 1881, granting legal rights to tenants, was just the first of a series of legislative successes that culminated in the Land Acts giving Irish farmers the right to buy out their land with low interest Government loans.

Parnell suffered a severe setback in 1882 when the new Irish cabinet secretary, Frederick Cavendish and his top civil servant, Thomas Henry Burke, were hacked to death outside the gates of the Viceregal Lodge, now Áras an Uachtaráin, by members of a secret society called the Invincibles. The brutal murder of the cabinet Minister responsible for Ireland tarnished the campaign for Home Rule for a time. Parnell even considered quitting politics until it became clear that neither he nor his party had anything whatever to do with the crime.

In the general election of 1885 Parnell's party won 85 seats. Discipline had been tightened considerably with every selected candidate signing a pledge to 'sit, act and vote' with the party or to resign their seat if they failed to honour the pledge. Party whips were appointed to ensure strict discipline. It was the first time that the Commons had experienced such tight political discipline and it changed the way the House did its business as the major British parties copied the Irish tactics. The strict political discipline introduced by Parnell remains a feature of Irish politics to this day with little or no dissent from the party line being tolerated by any of the major parties.

Parnell achieved the balance of power in 1885 and used it to put Gladstone's Liberals in power. Gladstone himself had become a convert to Home Rule and in 1886 introduced the First Home Rule Bill to the British Parliament. It was a move that split the Liberal Party and changed the face of British politics. Some of the great Whig nobles like Lord Hartington left the party of their forebears and so did a section of the new Liberal party headed by the dynamic businessman, Joseph Chamberlain. The Liberal Unionists joined with the Conservatives to defeat Gladstone's Home Rule Bill and drive him out of office.

It was a bitter, if unsurprising blow to Parnell's hopes. The following year his personal reputation was challenged by a series of letters to *The Times* that linked him to support for agrarian crime. The charges were ultimately exposed as a fraud by a special Commission in 1890 and Parnell appeared to be in a strong position to unite all shades of nationalist opinion in another push for Home Rule when the Liberals returned to office. However, his newly restored reputation did not last long.

In 1890 the Irish Parliamentary Party was torn apart when it emerged in the divorce courts that Parnell had been conducting a long-standing affair with a married woman, Katharine O'Shea. What made it all the more damaging was that Parnell had used his influence to have his lover's disreputable husband, Captain O'Shea, installed as an Irish Party MP for Galway. The traumatic split that followed the divorce has gone down in popular memory as a case of the moral majority deserting their embattled leader. In fact the majority of Irish MPs deserted their leader, not on moral grounds but on coldly pragmatic political considerations. The party came apart because its members were faced with a choice between their leader and their cause: between Parnell and Home Rule.

The sequence of events was that on 17 November 1890, Katharine O'Shea was divorced by her husband and Parnell cited as co-respondent. Immediately afterwards all the Liberal newspapers in London declared that Parnell's retirement from public life was inevitable. In Ireland the response was different. Nationalist newspapers were unanimously in favour of Parnell continuing as leader and on 20 November at a huge meeting in

Dublin attended by most of the leading nationalist politicians a resolution was passed pledging to stand by the leader.

In England, however, most of Gladstone's non-conformist supporters were strongly against Parnell on moral grounds and the pressure was too much for the Prime Minister to resist. On 24 November he delivered an ultimatum to the Irish Party that Parnell would have to retire if Home Rule was to stay on his agenda. On the same day, before they were made aware of the ultimatum, the Party MPs met at Westminster and unanimously re-elected Parnell as chairman.

Two days later, on the publication of Gladstone's letter, a number of senior figures like Justin McCarthy, Thomas Sexton and Tim Healy called on him to step down. More senior figures like John Dillon and William O'Brien were in the US but they also sided against their leader. The bishops now joined the anti-Parnell side and on 1 December a series of stormy meetings began in Committee Room 15 at Westminster. Violent speeches were made and it was evident that the majority was against Parnell. However, Parnell blocked every attempt to take a vote on a resolution calling on him to resign.

On 7 December the meetings in Committee Room 15 came to a crisis. Most of the senior figures opposed Parnell, with the exception of John Redmond, and the drama of the meetings is vividly captured in the *Freeman's Journal* verbatim reporting of proceedings. The most famous moment came when Redmond stood by his Chief.

'Mr J. Redmond: 'The master of the Party.' (cheers and counter cheers).

'Mr T. Healy: 'Who is to be the mistress of the Party?' (cries of shame, noise, several members calling out remarks which could not be distinguished in the uproar).

'Mr W. Redmond: 'They must be very badly off when they go to arguments like that.

'A Voice: 'It is true.'

'Mr A. O'Connor: 'I appeal to my friend the Chairman.' (noise).

'Mr Parnell: 'Better appeal to your own friends. Better appeal to that cowardly little scoundrel there (noise) that in an assembly of Irishmen dares to insult a woman.' (loud cheers and counter cheers).'

In the midst of the drama Parnell still refused to allow a vote on his leadership. A majority of MPs withdrew from the room and held an independent meeting of their own. The party was now split in two. Once the split had become formalised, the two factions began contesting by-election vacancies in Ireland in the spring and summer of 1891. Appalling things were said from pulpits and political platforms and Irish politics was soured for the next decade.

Parnell pushed himself to the limit travelling up and down the country and appealing for the support of nationalist voters but he couldn't stem the political tide. All he managed to do was to ruin his health in the process and he died on 6 October 1891, at the age of 45, leaving a divided party and a disillusioned electorate behind. In time the treatment of Parnell came to be widely regarded as a gross betrayal, and two of Ireland's greatest literary figures, Yeats and Joyce, immortalised that view. In Joyce's *Portrait of the Artist* the family row over Parnell at the Christmas dinner turned an incident from Irish politics into world literature. In 'Come Gather

Round Me, Parnellites' (*Last Poems*, 1935) Yeats summed up
the Parnell legend in ringing tones.

The Bishops and the Party
That tragic story made,
A husband that had sold his wife
And after that betrayed;
But stories that live longest
Are sung above the glass,
And Parnell loved his country,
And Parnell loved his lass.

RICHARD MARTIN (1754–1834)

Known as 'Humanity Dick', Martin came from one of the 'Tribes
of Galway' and was a member of a noted land-owning family.
From his family seat at Ballynahinch Castle he was virtually the
King of Connemara, where he had an estate that came to over
200,000 acres and stretched for 30 miles. After an education at
Harrow and Cambridge, Martin was elected to the Irish
Parliament in 1776. He served in the Parliament for the next 24
years but supported the Act of Union in 1800 that led to the
abolition of the Irish Parliament. He was subsequently elected
to the House of Commons for County Galway from 1800 to
1812, when he took a break from politics. He returned in the
general election of 1818 and while he was elected again in 1826
he was unseated on petition.

Martin was best known for his love of animals. In 1822 he
succeeded in pushing a Bill through the Commons that was the
first piece of legislation to protect the rights of domestic
animals. He was the driving force behind the foundation of the
Royal Society for the Prevention of Cruelty to Animals in 1824.
Also a noted duellist and liver of the good life, Martin's twin
passions came together as he regularly challenged those he
witnessed ill treating animals to fight him in a duel. 'Sir, an ox

cannot hold a pistol,' he once remarked.

Martin did not confine his attentions to the welfare of animals. In Parliament he supported Catholic Emancipation and tried to abolish the death penalty for forgery. He was known as a generous landlord. It was King George IV, a long-time personal friend, who christened him 'Humanity Dick'. After being deprived of his parliamentary seat and having run up huge debts, he retired to Boulogne where he died in 1834.

THE O'GORMAN MAHON (1800–1891)

One of the most colourful politicians ever to serve in the House of Commons, James Patrick O'Gorman Mahon was first elected to the unreformed Parliament of 1830 and was a serving MP when he died in 1891. He had a long and swashbuckling career as a soldier of fortune all over the globe and by his own account fought 13 duels, a number of which resulted in the death of his opponent.

Born into comfortable circumstances in Ennis, County Clare, he was educated at Trinity College Dublin. After graduation he joined the Catholic Association and played a prominent part in helping O'Connell to win the Clare election of 1828. Elected himself in 1830, O'Gorman Mahon was unseated on petition after allegations of bribery. O'Connell's son, Maurice, ran for Clare and beat O'Gorman Mahon for the second seat in the general election of 1831. This led to a quarrel between O'Gorman Mahon and O'Connell that never healed.

Disillusioned with Irish politics, he set out on a long tour of the world during which he served as an officer under the flags of France, Austria, Turkey and Russia in various wars. He returned home and stood for Ennis in 1847 and was elected unopposed. In 1852 he lost the seat by 13 votes and again set off for foreign fields. He served in the armies of various South American countries and took part in the American civil war. Although he served at various military ranks during his life as a soldier, he was known as 'the Major'.

He came back to Ireland in the 1870s and at the age of 79 was re-elected for Clare. Shortly afterwards he had the dubious honour of introducing Capt. O'Shea to Parnell, thus settingin motion the train of events that led to the famous divorce case. A genial mountain of a man, who relished his food and drink, he was a colourful and unconventional speaker and the Commons quickly filled when he got to his feet. O'Gorman and the tiny Nationalist MP, Joe Biggar, regularly acted as tellers for their party in divisions. 'Mr Biggar was a little hunchbacked man and to see him skipping up the House with the gigantic Major rolling astern, like a line of battle ship in the trough of the Atlantic, was a delight that never palled on the appetite of the House,' wrote one Victorian parliamentary sketch writer.

CHAPTER TWO

FROM HOME RULE TO THE RISING

Gladstone returned to power after the Parnell split and, true to his word, introduced a second Home Rule Bill in 1893. This time it passed through the Commons but was rejected by the House of Lords. The combination of this second defeat and the split in the Irish Party provoked considerable disillusionment with democratic politics in Ireland. The squabbling among politicians encouraged some energetic young nationalists to focus their energies on the Irish literary movement, the GAA or the more radical labour and socialist organisations that were springing up. The shadowy IRB had its tentacles in most of these movements, recruiting and encouraging revolution. Still, normal political activity went on and elections were hotly contested with supporters and opponents of Parnell slugging it out for mastery. Dublin, Waterford city and Clare remained fast to the memory of the chief but the rest of the country voted overwhelmingly for his enemies. In the general election of 1892 anti-Parnell Nationalists won 71 seats as against just 9 for the pro-Parnell faction.

After a decade of division the two factions came together again in 1900 under the leadership of John Redmond, the MP for Waterford city, who had sided with Parnell. Redmond, a native of Wexford from a prosperous farming background, was a barrister who started his working life as a clerk in the House of Commons. A fine speaker and a brilliant parliamentary tactician, colleagues found Redmond a reserved character. His over-riding political objective was to put the

Irish Party in a position to extract another Home Rule Bill from the British Government and he exercised great patience to achieve it. Known for his catchphrase 'wait and see' he was determined to keep his party disciplined and ready for the day when Home Rule would come back on the political agenda of a British Government.

That objective seemed very far off when Redmond took over the leadership because the Conservative Government of Lord Salisbury had an unassailable majority in the Commons. The Conservatives tried to take advantage of a weakened Irish nationalist movement by embarking on a policy that became known as 'killing Home Rule with kindness'. A series of Land Acts that enabled farmers to buy out their holdings, on ever more favourable terms, transferred the ownership of most agricultural land from landlords to tenants. A Department of Agriculture was established in Dublin to support Ireland's principal industry. It was headed by a Nationalist politician, TP Gill. A new local government act in 1898 established the county council system with a general council of county councils meeting once a year as a form of national assembly.

The more radical or 'advanced' nationalist politicians railed against Government's plans to sap the desire for Home Rule and tried to keep the spirit of agitation going in the country. The urbane writer, George Moore, described an 'advanced nationalist' of this period as: 'A politician who goes around the country encouraging small boys to throw large stones at the police.'

The Conservative party's domination of British politics collapsed in 1906 but it was now the Liberals who had a massive majority. Redmond still had no leverage although his

Liberal friends were in power and theoretically committed to Home Rule. In 1905 a new political movement called Sinn Féin was founded by the journalist and nationalist campaigner, Arthur Griffith, to push a more radical agenda than Home Rule. Based on the notion of national self-reliance, Sinn Féin advocated that Irish MPs should withdraw from Westminster and set up a parliament in Dublin. Griffith did not reject the British crown, as IRB republicans did. Instead he advocated a dual monarchy along the lines of the Austro-Hungarian Empire with each country recognising the same sovereign. Sinn Féin had some initial success in Dublin local elections but its first foray into national politics ended badly. The Irish Party MP for Leitrim North, Charles Dolan, resigned his seat at Westminster and announced his support for the Sinn Féin policy of abstention. He fought the subsequent by-election in 1908 but was out polled almost three to one by the Party candidate, Francis Meehan. It appeared to be the death knell for Sinn Féin as a national party and John Redmond announced: 'I have crushed Sinn Féin in the palm of my hand.'

At that stage Redmond was more concerned about another nationalist rival, the Cork MP, William O'Brien, who founded two popular grass-roots movements, the United Irish League and later the All For Ireland League. O'Brien was an anti-clerical maverick who sometimes condemned Redmond for being too moderate and at other times for being too extreme in pursuit of the national objective. O'Brien surprised everybody by staking his political fortunes on a deal with unionists based on the principles of 'conciliation and consent.' He was away ahead of his time with the consent principle but was denounced by Redmond for selling out on the holy grail of

Home Rule. O'Brien then set out to take control of Cork and the battle between his followers and those of Redmond, known locally as the All Fors and the Mollies, for dominance of Cork politics has been immortalised in literature by both Frank O'Connor and Seán O'Faolain. It was a battle O'Brien won in Cork although his band of eight MPs generally voted with the Irish Party in the Commons.

The general election of January 1910, catapulted constitutional nationalism back to the centre of British politics. Liberals and Conservatives finished in a dead heat. It meant that the Irish Party had the balance of power for the first time in two decades. The circumstances in which this came about was even more enticing for Redmond. The election was called because the House of Lords had rejected Lloyd George's People's Budget of 1909. This increased taxes on the rich and imposed a land tax. It also taxed publicans, alcoholic drink and motor cars. The budget was actually unpopular in Ireland because of the taxes on land and pubs. The publicans' lobby was as strong then as now and the Irish Party was widely known as the 'publicans and sinners' party. For Redmond, though, there was a much bigger issue at stake. By rejecting the Budget the Lords provoked the Liberal Government of Herbert Asquith to fury and he was determined to remove the veto exercise by the Upper House. That in turn would mean the Lords could not block Home Rule again.

When the election was called Redmond demanded a commitment by the Liberals to Home Rule. He threatened not only to withdraw support from Asquith after the election but also to call on Irish voters in England and Scotland to vote against the Liberals if the commitment was not forthcoming.

Asquith gave way and issued an election pledge that, if returned to office, the Liberal Government would set up a system of self-government in Ireland, for purely Irish affairs. The election result was everything that Redmond hoped for. The Liberals had 275 seats, the Conservatives 273, the Irish Party 82 and Labour 40. The way was open to abolish the Lords' veto. There was pressure from the King to get a compromise to avert a constitutional crisis but the Liberals and Conservatives failed to agree. When the Lords threatened to vote down any legislation passed by the Commons to remove their veto, Asquith proposed to create hundreds of new Liberal peers in order to get his Bill through. Before agreeing to cooperate the King insisted that Asquith would have to get a popular mandate for his plan, so a second election was called. This election in December 1910 produced an identical result so Redmond still had the balance of power. Faced with the prospect of being swamped by newly created peers the Lords acquiesced in the abolition of their veto. As 1911 dawned with the way cleared for Home Rule the road ahead looked rosy for nationalist Ireland.

However, Redmond, like Parnell before him, ignored one massive obstruction on that road. Irish Protestants were overwhelmingly opposed to Home Rule and in north-east Ulster, where they were in a majority, they were determined to resist it at all costs. That aspiration was fully supported by the Conservative Party which embarked on a potentially treasonous course to stop Home Rule becoming a reality. In Ireland the Ulster Unionists Council, established in 1905, banded the opponents of Home Rule into a formidable political organisation under the direction of James Craig.

While the two elections of 1910 demonstrated the determination of nationalist Ireland to secure Home Rule they also demonstrated the strength of resistance to that policy in the north-east of the country. In February 1910 the Irish Unionists asked one of the leading legal figures in the UK, Edward Carson, to be their parliamentary leader in the Commons. Carson, a Dublin Protestant and a brilliant lawyer, represented Trinity College in the Commons, 1892-1918. He made his way to the forefront of British politics, serving as solicitor general of Ireland and then England before the Conservative defeat of 1906. He was a charismatic and dashing figure who embodied the contradiction at the heart of resistance to Home Rule. He was so committed to the defence of the Union that he was prepared to subvert the British constitution to obtain his objective.

In 1911 the Lords's veto was removed and replaced by a three-year delaying power. In 1912 the third Home Rule Bill was finally introduced by the Liberal Government and extraordinary passions were released on all sides. Ireland was brought to the verge of a civil war and British democracy tottered on the edge of a precipice from which it was only saved by the outbreak of the First World War. The Home Rule Bill itself was a relatively modest proposal. It provided for an Irish Parliament to run local affairs but taxation and foreign policy were to be the preserve of the Government in London.

Modest proposal though it was, Home Rule provoked a ferocious reaction from unionists. The Ulster Volunteer Force (UVF) was formed to resist the measure and arms imported from Britain's great enemy Germany. More astonishingly the Conservative opposition backed the resistance movement to the hilt. Redmond and Asquith were initially unperturbed and maintained that the measure would become law regardless. Winston Churchill, the then Liberal Home Secretary, travelled to Belfast to speak in favour of Home Rule. He was welcomed at a public meeting in Celtic Park, on the Falls Road but there was widespread rioting in Protestant areas and the city centre. Ironically, Churchill's father, Randolph, had helped foment Unionist opposition to the First Home Rule Bill in 1886 warning: 'Ulster will fight; Ulster will be right.'

In the summer of 1912 Redmond brought Asquith to Dublin to show him the intensity of the passion for Home Rule. The Prime Minister received a tumultuous reception on his arrival in the Irish capital. When he stood up to speak at a public meeting in the Theatre Royal the Prime Minister was cheered for five solid minutes and the audience sang 'For He's a Jolly Good Fellow'. In his address Asquith dismissed all idea of civil war and said he would not be deterred from introducing Home Rule. Replying, Redmond said that Home Rule would be accepted by Ireland in absolute good faith as a final settlement of the quarrel between the two countries.

The Prime Minister's visit, though, suffered disruption from an unlikely source. A band of suffragettes, campaigning for the right of women to vote, travelled over from England ahead of him. The small group of suffragettes occupied a box in the dress circle of the Theatre Royal and attempted to start a fire during the meeting but it was quickly put out by members of the audience. The three then decided to make a spectacular protest at a procession through the city centre by Asquith and Redmond the following night. The procession started after dinner at which Asquith drank his customary bottle or more of good claret. Travelling in an open carriage, with his wife Margo and John Redmond, the Prime Minister appeared (to many in the crowd that lined the streets) to be nicely tipsy. The chief marshal walked alongside the carriage decked out resplendently in a Robert Emmet costume of green and gold. The procession became more exotic when Asquith's carriage was suddenly surrounded by a body of horsemen carrying torches. They were Dublin jarveys campaigning against the introduction of motor taxis to the city who had just dumped Dublin's first motor taxi into the Liffey. The unexpected involvement of the jarveys drew great applause from the crowd but more excitement was to follow. Near the GPO, Mary Leigh, the leader of the suffragette unit, dashed from the pavement and jumped up on to the back of the carriage. She was waving a brand new hatchet, which she proceeded to fling at the Prime Minister's head. Asquith was oblivious to the commotion and swayed out of the way as the hatchet shot past. It caught the unfortunate Redmond on the ear and cut him badly. Leigh jumped off the carriage and was grabbed by the chief marshal, but she showed her mettle by beating him in the face and then pulling the epaulettes off his fancy costume before escaping through the hostile crowd. She was arrested at her lodgings the following day.

Mary Leigh and her companions were sentenced to five years in prison for their actions and were incarcerated in Mountjoy Jail in Dublin. They promptly went on hunger strike and were then forcibly fed by the authorities. The Chief Secretary for Ireland, Augustine Birrell, who himself had been physically assaulted by suffragettes, wrote facetiously to his private secretary: 'I see no way out but either to kill these ladies by continued torture or to let them out to kill me.' Leigh and her friends were quickly released because of ill health and the embarrassment caused to the government.

The small but vibrant Irish suffragette movement a backlash from the hatchet affair and apples were thrown at speakers addressing a meeting calling for votes for women a few nights later. Women had been given the vote in the local government elections of 1898 but were still prohibited from voting in parliamentary elections. The Irish Women's Suffrage and Local Government Association started in 1901 but it was not until 1908 and the foundation of the Irish Women's Franchise League by Hanna Sheehy-Skeffington and Margaret Cousins that the movement made an impact on the political scene.

Like their counterparts in England, Irish suffragettes engaged in acts of civil disobedience. Window breaking emerged as the preferred tactic, and small carpenters' hammers soon became the symbolic fashion accessory of the suffragette movement. Although fashionable shop fronts along Dublin's Grafton and Sackville Streets were popular targets for this activity, Cousins believed in taking things straight to the heart of the political system, and began her personal campaign by daringly breaking windows in Dublin Castle. For her 'panes', as journalistic punsters had it, she was jailed for six months at Tullamore Prison. There she joined three other Suffragist prisoners in a six-day hunger strike. Hanna Sheehy-Skeffington was the most prominent Irish suffragettes whose father, David Sheehy, was an Irish Party MP. She was one of the first of a new generation of women to graduate from an Irish university. In June 1903 she married Francis Skeffington (1878–1916), a prominent and controversial journalist

with socialist and pacifist sympathies who was murdered
during the 1916 Rising.

After the commotion caused by his visit to Dublin Asquith
went ahead and pushed the Home Rule Bill through the House
of Commons. It was duly defeated in the Lords in 1912 but
with the ending of the veto it only had to pass twice more
through the Commons in order to become law. That made
1914 the deadline for the introduction of the measure.
However, the Liberal Government gradually came around to
the view that it would be impossible to impose Home Rule on
the whole island. Despite Redmond's furious opposition
Asquith and his Ministers decided that they had no option but
to consider partition. This view hardened after the Curragh
mutiny in the spring of 1914 when it became clear that
elements of the Army would refuse to impose Home Rule in
Ulster when the Bill became law later in that year. By that stage
nationalist Ireland had responded to the militancy of Ulster
with the formation of the National Volunteers. Founded by
Eoin MacNeill, the Volunteers sought to emulate the UVF and
also imported guns from Germany. Alarmed by the
development Redmond and the Party took control of the
Volunteers, but the real militants in the organisation were
agents of the IRB who bided their time until they could seize
control.

In May 1914 the Home Rule Bill passed through the
Commons for the third time but there was one important
caveat. The Government had come to the conclusion that
provision would have to be made for separate treatment for
some, or all, of Ulster. Its first approach was to propose a
'county option' under which the Ulster countries and the

boroughs of Belfast and Derry would each be given the choice of whether they wanted to opt out of Home Rule for a specified period. The British cabinet pored over maps of Ulster, with Asquith and Churchill becoming more familiar than they ever wanted to be with the parishes of Fermanagh and Tyrone. It was generally accepted that on the basis of the 1911 census only four Ulster counties: Armagh, Antrim, Derry and Down, were likely to opt out. Redmond reluctantly accepted county option as the only means of getting the Bill through – but it was rejected by the Ulster Unionists.

Full-scale civil war in Ireland and a constitutional crisis for the whole UK loomed and in July King George V called a constitutional conference at Buckingham Palace to see if a solution could be found on the basis of the exclusion of some or all of Ulster. The leaders of the Liberals and Conservatives, Unionists and Nationalists met for weeks but failed to reach agreement. Redmond would not go beyond county option and temporary exclusion, which effectively meant four counties would be excluded for six years. Carson and Craig insisted on permanent exclusion of six counties. It was at the Buckingham Palace conference that the germ of partition on the basis of a six-county state emerged.

Meanwhile, an event that had already taken place in Sarajevo in Bosnia was to sweep the Irish issue and the prospect of partition away from the centre of British politics. The assassination of the Austrian Archduke, Franz Ferdinand, by a Serb militant set off a chain of events that culminated in the German invasion of Belgium and France and the beginning of the First World War in August.

Despite the failure to reach an agreement at the Buckingham

Palace conference, the Home Rule Bill was enacted but suspended until the end of the war with a commitment from Asquith that it would not be implemented without amendment to take account of the Ulster problem. When the war started Redmond came to a momentous decision aimed at delivering a 32-county Home Rule at the War's end.

After the Foreign Secretary, Edward Grey, made his famous speech in the Commons about 'the lamps going out all over Europe', Redmond intervened in the debate:

Today there are in Ireland two large bodies of Volunteers. One of them sprang into existence in the North. Another sprang into existence in the South. I say to the Government that they may tomorrow withdraw every one of their troops from Ireland. I say that the coast of Ireland will be defended from foreign invasion by her armed sons, and for this purpose armed Nationalist Catholics in the South will only be too glad to join arms with the armed Protestant Ulstermen in the North.

The speech electrified the Commons and Redmond was applauded on all sides. If he had left it at that, all might have been well, but a month later he went a step further. In September 1914, when the Home Rule Act was formally placed on the statute book he made a speech at Woodenbridge in County Wicklow pledging the Volunteers to the war effort.

The war is undertaken in the defence of the highest principles of religion and morality and right and it would be a disgrace for ever to our country, and a reproach to her manhood, and a denial of the lessons of her history, if young Ireland confined their efforts to remaining at home to defend the shores of Ireland from an unlikely invasion.

The belief that involvement in the war would lead to Irish unity was clearly a strong motivating factor in Redmond's call to arms, but it was not the only one. Like many middle-class Irish nationalists he was appalled at the atrocities perpetrated by the Imperial German army on the Catholic people of Belgium in the early days of the war. His niece, who was a nun in Belgium, gave him a first-hand account of the suffering inflicted on the population and he was deeply moved.

Redmond also believed that, by defending the right of a small nation like Belgium to exist against the power of Prussian totalitarianism, Irish soldiers would vindicate the right of freedom for their own country.

I am speaking the truth when I say of the Irish race as a whole that they would feel covered with humiliation if when this war is over they had to admit that their rights and liberties had been saved by the sacrifices of other men while Irishmen remained safe at home and took no risks,' he said. He also fatally underestimated the potential of his opponents dismissing Sinn Féin as 'a handful of pro-German shirkers.

If the war had ended in a few months, as all the experts predicted at the time, Redmond's tactics might have had some chance of working. Of course, far from ending, the War went on and on and the carnage of the western front cast Redmond's encouragement to enlist in a very different light. The Woodenbridge speech marked a political disaster for Redmond and it ultimately destroyed his reputation, his party, and the policy to which he had devoted his life.

The first thing that happened was that the Volunteers split. Redmond initially held on to the vast majority with 150,000 nominal members compared to the 5000 or so who left to form the new Irish Volunteers. Eoin Mac Neill led the breakaway group, but more significantly, the IRB dominated its executive. As the War dragged on Redmond's National Volunteers declined, through enlistment or demoralisation, while the Irish Volunteers flourished, joining with Sinn Féin in opposing recruitment and ultimately supporting the German cause.

In 1915 the British political situation changed with the creation of a coalition Government to prosecute the war. Asquith was still prime minister but the pro-Irish Liberals were no longer in control. The Ulster Unionist leader, Carson, joined the cabinet and became an influential member. Asquith did offer a cabinet post to Redmond but he refused to accept it in the belief that it would undermine his authority as the leader of Irish nationalism.

Redmond was undoubtedly right in his assessment, but his position was undermined in any case. Although he had achieved a political victory by having all of Ireland excluded from the imposition of conscription, the public became steadily more disenchanted with the war as it dragged on through 1915 and into 1916.

Then in 1916 came the Rising that changed the political situation utterly. The Rising was the project of a minority within a minority. The plot was devised by a select band of IRB militants without the knowledge of the wider IRB and in defiance of MacNeill's authority. The Rising was far from being a popular revolt but the destruction of Dublin, the courage of its leaders and most importantly of all, the executions that followed its defeat, turned the tide of public opinion in the aftermath.

The Easter Rising marked the end of Redmond's authority. As the *London Times* noted at the time, the Sinn Féin movement 'from the first was directed as much against Mr Redmond and the nationalist Party as against Great Britain.' Redmond was shattered by the Rising which came as much of a surprise to him as to the British Government. He pleaded with Asquith in the House of Commons for restraint and rightly forecast that the executions' policy would make martyrs of the rebels. His advice was ignored and the prediction he had feared came to pass.

After the Rising the British explored the possibility of the immediate introduction of Home Rule with some form of Ulster exclusion to settle the situation. Asquith asked Lloyd George to negotiate with the Irish leaders. The wily Welshman managed to persuade Redmond to agree to six-county exclusion on the basis that it would be subject to review after the War. Simultaneously, he assured Carson that exclusion would be permanent. Disagreements in the British cabinet prevented the plan from being implemented but it marked a firming up of the idea of six-county exclusion.

After the fruitless talks a series of by-elections in 1917 demonstrated just how badly damaged Redmond and his party had been when supporters of the Rising defeated the Irish Party candidates. The first to be elected in February 1917, was Count Plunkett, father of the executed 1916 leader, Joseph Mary Plunkett. He was supported by republicans but was not formally a Sinn Féin candidate and had to be actively persuaded not to take his seat in the House of Commons.

The next by-election of May 1917, in Longford South was an even more serious contest for the future of Ireland. The Irish Party threw everything into the defence of the seat while the Sinn Féin candidate was Joe McGuinness, who was still in jail for his part in the Rising. 'Put him in to get him out' was the famous slogan of the rebels. There was bedlam in Longford on the day of the count with an initial announcement that the Party candidate, Joseph McKenna, had won only for it to be retracted and McGuinness declared the victor by 30 votes. The returning officer claimed the result had changed because an uncounted parcel of votes had been found but there were also allegations that a gunman had threatened violence if McGuinness was not declared the winner.

In July Eamon de Valera, the only surviving commandant from the Rising, had a decisive victory in Clare. That was a truly bitter blow for Redmond as the by-election was held to fill the vacancy caused by the death of his brother, Willie, who had been killed fighting on the western front.

Meanwhile Redmond suffered further humiliation. Another attempted initiative by the British Government was the establishment of the Irish Convention of 1917. Like so many attempts at a political solution before and since, the efforts of moderate nationalists and unionists to find an accommodation foundered as Sinn Féin boycotted the proceedings and Ulster unionists insisted on permanent partition.

Redmond was physically assaulted by a group of young Sinn Féiners while walking along Westmoreland Street on his way to the Convention. It was a demonstration of just how much the rules of democratic politics had been undermined.

John Redmond died prematurely at the age of 62 in March 1918 knowing that his political life had ended in failure. His dream of a united Ireland with its own parliament living in a harmonious relationship with the UK was destroyed by a combination of Unionists, Republicans and the British Conservative Party. It was to take another 80 years before the political leaders of Ireland and Britain arrived at a settlement that would put the relationship between the countries on a truly harmonious footing. By then a lot of blood had flowed under the bridge and Redmond's memory had almost been forgotten.

ARTHUR MACMORROUGH KAVANAGH (1831–1889)

A remarkable man for his own or any other era, Arthur MacMorrough Kavanagh was born in Borris, County Carlow, to one of the oldest land-owning families in the country. What was extraordinary about him was that he was born virtually without arms or legs, having only rudimentary limbs in their place. Despite this disability he learned to ride, shoot and fish and became a reasonably good painter, using his arms with dexterity. He rode to hounds strapped to a chair saddle.

After travelling to India and Russia as a young man he returned to Borris in 1853 and succeeded to the family estates at the age of 22. He rebuilt the towns of Borris and Ballyragget and subsidised a railway line from Borris to Bagnelstown.

A Protestant, Kavanagh was elected as a Conservative MP for Wexford in 1866 and at the next election transferred to Carlow where he was MP from 1868 to 1880. The widening of the franchise and the rise of the Home Rule movement put an end to his political career and he lost his seat in the election of 1880. He was a frequent contributor in the Commons during his time in parliament.

MICHAEL DAVITT (1846–1906)

One of the great figures of Irish history, Michael Davitt probably had more impact on the lives of ordinary Irish people than any other political figure in pre-Independence Ireland. He, more than anybody else, created the conditions whereby the land of Ireland was transferred from the landlord class to the tenant farmers. Ironically, Davitt became a believer in land nationalisation but his successful campaign created a conservative, owner-occupying rural society.

Born in Straide, County Mayo, Davitt's family emigrated to Lancashire when he was four-years-old, following their eviction from their small farm. He lost his right arm in a factory accident working as a child labourer in a cotton mill. In 1865 he joined the Fenians and was sentenced to 15 years in prison in 1870 for gunrunning.

Davitt was released from Dartmoor after seven years, mainly because of agitation by Parnell and Issac Butt. He went to the US, where in cooperation with John Devoy, he worked out a new policy for the national movement based on the twin aims of self-government and land reform. Known as 'the new departure' this policy united nationalists of all shades from IRB revolutionaries to constitutional politicians.

Davitt came back to Ireland in 1879 as crop failure and falling prices left the rural population facing disaster. He persuaded Parnell to speak at a huge meeting in Westport at which the Irish Party leader uttered the famous words: 'Hold a firm grip of your homesteads and lands.' Four months later Davitt founded the Land League and, following mass agitation up and down the country, the result was a succession of Land Acts that paved the way for the transfer of the land of Ireland from the landlords to the farmers.

Davitt was elected as a MP in 1882 but his increasing

interest in land nationalisation led to an open breach with Parnell. One of his proposals, vetoed by Parnell, was that one of the leaders of the Indian independence movement be given a safe nationalist seat in Ireland to press for his country's cause in the House of Commons. Davitt took the anti-Parnell side during the split. He left politics in 1899 and devoted himself to writing and agitation.

CHAPTER THREE

FROM THE FIRST DÁIL
TO CIVIL WAR

When the First World War ended in November 1918, the British Prime Minister, Lloyd George, dissolved Parliament and called a general election. The timing was dictated by Lloyd George's own political ends but it was the opportunity Sinn Féin was waiting for.

The organisation was very different from when it was founded in 1905.

Arthur Griffith, founder of the party, was not a republican and did not advocate the use of violence to achieve independence. The British mistakenly called the 1916 Rising: the Sinn Féin Rebellion.

Although Sinn Féin members like WT Cosgrave had taken part in the Rising the real leaders were IRB republican separatists.

When those arrested in the aftermath of the Rising were released in 1917 they came home to a changed country. Sinn Féin became the vehicle for the expression of the changed national mood with radical republicans joining Griffith's original members to create what was effectively a new party that Griffith no longer controlled. At a convention in October 1917, Griffith was persuaded to stand down as party president. Eamon de Valera, the new MP for Clare, took over the top position while Griffith accepted the post of vice president. From the start there were obvious strains between the more militant republicans and the supporters of the old non-violent abstentionist policy. The wording of the reconstituted party's aims reflected this ambiguity. 'Sinn Féin aims at securing the international recognition of Ireland as an independent Irish republic. Having achieved that status the Irish people may by referendum freely choose their own form of government.'

It was the prospect of conscription in 1918 that made the Sinn Féin tide unstoppable. In April 1918 Lloyd George had produced legislation that threatened to extend conscription to Ireland. The reaction was immediate with all shades of nationalist opinion from Sinn Féin to the weakened Irish Party forming a popular front in opposition to the measure. The Catholic Church and the trade union movement endorsed the anti-conscription campaign and there was a one-day general strike outside Ulster. Sinn Féin, as the party that had opposed the War from the very beginning, reaped all the political benefits and it was transformed into a national political movement. By December 1918 the party had 112,080 registered members and when the election was called the only issue was how big the Sinn Féin mandate was going to be. The Irish Party struggled to find candidates in a number of constituencies. Many sitting MPs simply threw in the towel rather than face popular rejection, while others did not have the heart to brave the intimidating atmosphere generated by the rise of Sinn Féin. The embryonic Labour Party, which was just six years old, decided not to contest the election. The ostensible reason was that it did not wish to split the Sinn Féin vote, but in reality it had a limited organisation and just a handful of prospective candidates.

An important development was that the franchise was widened significantly in 1918. For the first time all adult males over 21 were allowed to vote, with no property qualification required. Women got the vote for the first time with the restriction that it only applied to those over the age of 30. More than two thirds of the electorate were first-time voters and this reinforced the mood for change. The result was a landslide: Sinn Féin won 73 seats as against just 6 for the Irish Party. A few Irish Party MPs survived in Ulster because of the nationalist fear of dividing the vote and allowing a Unionist slip in. Waterford city did remain true to its lost leader, John Redmond, electing his son Capt. Willie Redmond, but the Irish Party was effectively replaced by Sinn Féin in December 1918 as the national political movement.

However, as at the time of O'Connell's triumph in 1832 or Parnell's in 1885, nationalist Ireland ignored one glaringly obvious fact: the Protestants of Ulster once again rejected the nationalist agenda in an equally emphatic fashion. Unionists won 26 of the 105 Irish seats, almost all of them concentrated in Ulster. Southern unionism did pull off one victory with Maurice E. Dockrell, taking a seat in Rathmines to join the MP for Trinity College in the Commons. All of the other Unionist MPs were elected in the North and their determination to remain in the UK remained stead fast.

The Sinn Féin programme stressed that the party's MPs would not take their seats at Westminster but would instead set up an alternative parliament in Ireland. An appeal was promised to the post-war peace conference at Versailles with particular emphasis on the words of US President Wilson that no people should be forced to live under the sovereignty of a state to which it did not wish to belong. The party also promised resistance to British power by 'any and every means.'

PEOPLE, POLITICS AND POWER

The IRB was influential in selecting Sinn Féin candidates and organising the campaign but the party included a broad range of views and consciously projected itself as a national movement spanning all class interests. In the countryside some Sinn Féin candidates encouraged landless men to seize the property of the big farmers or graziers while others represented the interests of those same farmers.

On 21 January 1919 the newly elected Sinn Féin MPs met in the Mansion House and constituted themselves as an independent Irish parliament which they called the First Dáil. Many of the leading figures of the movement like de Valera, Griffith and WT Cosgrave were in jail or on the run and were unable to attend the first meeting. In the absence of more senior figures the 30 or so MPs in attendance elected Cathal Brugha as the acting president or Príomh Aire. They also titled themselves Teachta Dála (TD) rather than members of parliament. When the Dáil met for the second time on 1 April de Valera, who had escaped from Lincoln Jail, took over from Brugha as president. He appointed Griffith as vice president and Minister for Home Affairs; Michael Collins, the rising star of the movement was made Minister for Finance; Plunkett was given responsibility for Foreign Affairs; MacNeill got Industry; Cosgrave, Local Government; Brugha, Defence, and Countess Markievicz was Minister for Labour.

On the day the First Dáil met in January another incident took place that was to have a profound effect on Irish politics. At Soloheadbeg, County Tipperary, a group of Volunteers led by Dan Breen attacked and killed two policemen, beginning a guerrilla war that was to operate in parallel with the activities of the Dáil. The Soloheadbeg ambush shocked public opinion across the political divide and the killings were denounced from the pulpit in the local parish church. Griffith was not happy about the killings and some of the other leaders were very uneasy.

Eamon de Valera was self-confident, intelligent, legalistic, long-winded and austere. He was a reserved figure but his remoteness created a mystique around him as it had with Parnell. Born to an Irish mother and a Spanish father in New York, he was brought home by his mother at an early age and reared by his grandparents in Bruree, County Limerick. His American birth helped save him from execution in 1916 and his status as the senior surviving commandant helped propel him to the leadership of the national movement. He did not remain in Ireland for long after his election as president of the Dáil, but was smuggled off to the USA to campaign for Irish independence. Because of President Wilson's declaration in favour of small nations, the US was seen as the key to international recognition of the Dáil.

In America de Valera was welcomed by the legendary Fenian leader, John Devoy, who had campaigned tirelessly in the US for Irish independence and was a thorn in the side of the British Government. However, relations between de Valera and Devoy soon deteriorated in a struggle for control of the independence movement in America. It was a tussle that occupied the time of both men and ultimately ended in a complete break between them.

With de Valera out of Ireland for over a year, Griffith, as the acting president, focused on the original Sinn Féin plan of trying to create an independent state by simply refusing to recognise British authority. The Minister for Local

Government, the experienced Dublin local politician, WT Cosgrave, persuaded many county councils to recognise the Dáil as the legitimate government of Ireland rather than the British administration. Sinn Féin courts were set up as an alternative justice system and the Dáil raised a substantial loan to fund its operations with the Minister for Finance, Michael Collins, showing a flair for financial matters. Collins rose through the ranks of the conspiratorial IRB and had put himself in a pivotal position by 1918. As well as being a Dáil Minister he was the IRA's director of Intelligence, he was widely credited with masterminding the campaign of assassination against the police that helped to undermine British rule and provoke a violent counter reaction that worked to the advantage of the separatists. The opposite of de Valera in temperament, Collins was sociable, rumbustious, ruthless and very much one of the lads. He had a natural flair for self promotion and while his reputation grew as a gunman it was his political ability in the widest sense of the word that propelled him to the front rank of the movement.

The combined activities of the Dáil and the Volunteers, who soon became known as the Irish Republican Army (IRA) left the British Government in a quandary. It alternated between repressive measures like the introduction of the Black and Tans, special courts and curfews, but it also engaged in back channel communications hinting that it was prepared to negotiate with Sinn Féin. On the Irish side there were also contradictions. The IRA tactic of killing policemen, often when they were off duty and unarmed, horrified many people including some members of Sinn Féin. A clear gulf began to open up between those who favoured political action and those in the IRA who regarded politics as 'unclean' and violence as 'pure.' The IRA began to regard itself as the soul of the independence movement whose duty it was to stop the politicians selling out on the republic.

The divided state of Irish public opinion was illustrated in local government elections in urban areas that were held in January 1920. In an attempt to clip Sinn Féin's wings the British Government introduced the single transferable vote (STV) system of proportional representation instead of the first past the post system for these elections. The results certainly showed that the political map of Ireland was more complex than the 1918 result had indicated. Sinn Féin was the biggest party in urban Ireland with 27% of the vote closely followed by the Unionists with 26%. Labour took 18%, the Irish Party hung on to 15% and Independents won 14%. Subsequent county council elections in June were much better for Sinn Féin with the party winning majorities in 29 out of the 33 county councils. Sinn Féin was strongest in rural areas, particularly in the west and south and weakest in urban areas, particularly in Belfast.

The British response to the chaotic state of Ireland was the Government of Ireland Act of December 1920. This legislation superceded the Home Rule Act and provided for separate parliaments for Northern and Southern Ireland. The cabinet committee, chaired by the Conservative, Walter Long, which drafted the Act, recommended partition on a nine-county basis. This was overruled by the full cabinet, under pressure from Craig, who feared that the survival of a nine-county state could not be guaranteed in the long term because a Catholic majority might emerge. The paradox of the settlement was that it was immediately embraced by the Unionists, who had fought against Home Rule for so long, but rejected by nationalists who now wanted much more.

Elections to both parliaments were held in May 1921 under PR (STV). In the North, Unionists obtained the expected decisive majority. A small number of Sinn Féin and Nationalist MPs were elected but anti-Catholic pogroms that erupted in response to the IRA campaign in the region weakened the opposition to Unionism. In the South not a single constituency was actually contested. Sinn Féin simply nominated the relevant number of candidates to fill all the seats in each constituency and they were returned unopposed. The Northern Parliament was officially opened by King George V and while the Sinn Féin and Nationalist members stayed away the King made a conciliatory speech pleading for a settlement in the rest of Ireland.

Lloyd George followed up with an offer to negotiate with Sinn Féin and a truce between the IRA and the Crown forces was called in July 1921. Negotiations opened between de Valera and Lloyd George and were followed by detailed talks at Downing Street between a delegation from the Dáil and the leading members of the British Government including Lloyd George, Churchill and Lord Birkenhead. De Valera refused to go to London for the substantive talks and the delegation was led by Griffith and Collins. This move puzzled contemporaries and historians alike. At the time Collins told the Dáil that de Valera should lead the talks team and so did Cosgrave who said it made no sense to leave 'their ablest player in reserve.'

The Dáil delegation spent two months in intensive negotiations with the British before terms were agreed amid high drama. The British initially offered dominion status, akin to that of

Canada, while the Dáil delegation attempted to get something closer to a republic. The result was a compromise that conferred independence in most things, including finance and foreign policy – but it did not deliver the republic. Ireland would have to remain part of the Empire and be titled a Free State. Most controversially of all, an oath of fidelity to the British Crown would still be required from elected politicians and senior servants of the state. The negotiators did manage to water down the Oath. Every elected member of the Dáil would be required to swear allegiance not to the Crown but to the constitution of the Free State. They would also have to express fidelity to the King in virtue of the common citizenship of the two islands. Partition, which had already been institutionalised by the Government of Ireland Act, would be looked at by a boundary commission. This idea was devised initially by Lloyd George as a means of putting pressure on Craig but the Prime Minister then came to regard it as a solution to the Ulster problem. He persuaded Griffith and subsequently Collins to accept it. They both did on the assumption that the Free State would get Fermanagh, Tyrone, Derry city and substantial parts of Down and Derry and that such a loss of territory would make Northern Ireland unworkable as a political entity.

The delegation signed the Treaty without consulting de Valera but he rejected it immediately on their return to Ireland. The compromise on sovereignty, particularly the recognition of the Crown, was at the heart of the opposition to the Treaty, not partition as is often assumed. There was a rancorous cabinet meeting at which the Treaty was approved by four votes to three with Cosgrave backing the delegates Griffith, Collins and Barton against de Valera, Brugha and Austin Stack.

The issue was then referred to the Dáil which debated the issue in Earlsfort Terrace, now the National Concert Hall. The debate went on from 14 December 1921 until 10 January 1922 and there were passionate speeches on all sides. Many TDs were confused to find de Valera and Collins on what appeared to be the wrong sides. Dev as the leading politician in the Dáil had been the one that the more militant TDs expected to 'sell out' on the republic. Collins because of his reputation as the leader of the 'gunman' was expected by many to stand by the republic. Broadly speaking the old Sinn Féin, as represented by Griffith and Cosgrave, supported the Treaty while most of those associated with the IRA campaign opposed it.

De Valera confused his supporters by introducing an alternative to the Treaty, called: Document Number 2. This was based on the concept of external association with the Empire and it did not appear to his colleagues to be all that different from the Treaty. He spoke at length in the Dáil debates arguing for his solution and ignoring the fact that it had already been rejected out of hand by the British negotiators. Collins made shorter and more cogent speeches arguing that while the Treaty was not the ideal solution it was the best available and gave Ireland the freedom to achieve full freedom.

When the vote was taken the Treaty was passed by a slim majority of 64 votes to 57. De Valera resigned as president of the Dáil and was replaced by Griffith on 10 January. On 12 January Griffith summoned the members of the House of Commons of Southern Ireland, elected under the Government of Ireland Act (identical with the membership of the Second Dáil). Only the pro-Treaty TDs attended and Collins was elected chairman of a Provisional Government whose job it was to prepare the way for the implementation of the Treaty. The political situation was horribly confused with a Dáil headed by Griffith, a Provisional Government headed by Collins and a large dissenting minority in the Dáil headed by de Valera.

Griffith and Collins were determined that the people would be given the chance to make the final decision on the Treaty either through a referendum or a general election. An election was initially planned for the spring of 1922 but it was postponed because of republican objections and also because the new administration was busy working on a constitution for the new state. Collins attempted to drop the Oath from the constitution but the British insisted that it remain. In an effort to avoid civil war, and to ensure that the election would not be disrupted by the IRA, Collins made a controversial decision to enter an electoral pact with de Valera. This provided for the return of pro- and anti-Treaty factions of Sinn Féin to the Dáil in their existing strength and the formation of a coalition government in which five cabinet posts should go to the pro-Treaty group and four to the anti-Treaty faction. Griffith was appalled at the pact, particularly as public opinion appeared to be strongly pro-Treaty. Collins, however, thought it was a price worth paying to have a reasonably free and fair election. A fatal flaw in the pact was that PR in multi-seat constituencies would undermine its effectiveness if other non-Sinn Féin candidates entered the race.

The anti-Treaty faction recognised the threat and tried to intimidate non-Sinn Féin candidates out of the election. Labour braved the storm, insisting on its right to run and so did the Farmers Party. Former Home Rulers and Independents of all hues also got in on the act. All of these parties and groups made it clear they accepted the Treaty. The Labour Party has never received the credit it deserves for standing by democracy at this time!

Dan Morrissey, a Labour candidate in Tipperary, showed the kind of courage that was necessary to contest that election. He was ordered by the IRA not to stand but secretly left his home in Nenagh the night before nominations closed and made his way to Thurles.

He got through the crowds outside the courthouse without being recognised and managed to hand in his nomination papers. Word spread quickly and when he came back out into the square he was surrounded by hostile republicans. Ernie O'Malley, one of the ideologues of the IRA, took out a revolver put it to Morrissey's head and told him to go back inside and withdraw his nomination. Although he feared he was going to be killed Morrissey refused. At that moment one of the best-known IRA men in the country, Dan Breen, stepped forward, put a gun to O'Malley's head and told him that he would die if he shot Morrissey. O'Malley quickly put his gun down. Although Breen was on the republican side and had fought with O'Malley, he was from the same parish as Morrissey and they had distant ties of kinship. That counted for more than ideology with Breen, who was the only candidate in the election standing for both the pro- and anti-treaty sides. Shots were subsequently fired into Morrissey's house during the campaign but he had the satisfaction of being elected to the Dáil.

Under the terms of the Collins-de Valera pact Tipperary's seven seats had been allocated four:three in favour of the

Treaty side. However, 15 candidates put themselves forward and the result was that three pro-Treaty, two anti-Treaty, one Labour and one Farmers candidates were elected. Similar results were repeated all over the country. There were also similar levels of intimidation. Just to show how confused the political situation was, Dan Breen, who was standing for election in the Waterford-Tipperary constituency was allegedly involved in intimidating a Farmers Party candidate, who was subsequently shot and wounded and withdrew from the contest. Similar incidents happened around the country as candidates withdrew from the race when their lives were threatened and their families intimidated. Canvassers for the smaller parties were routinely beaten up and one Independent, Darrell Figgis, had to endure the indignity of having his beard shaved off in public by republicans who wanted him to withdraw. He got his revenge by topping the poll in Dublin County. Republican intimidation worked to the extent that 7 of the 27 constituencies were not contested but the 20 that did see a contest ensured that the pact failed.

It took almost a week to complete the count but the result was decisive. In the 122 member Third Dáil the Pro-Treaty Sinn Féin candidates won 40% of the vote, the anti-Treaty slate won 20% while the other 40% went to a range of pro-Treaty parties with Labour taking almost 20%. Collins appeared to repudiate the pact two days before the election but it became irrelevant in any case when the voters effectively threw it out. Republicans maintained at the time, and since, that the election could not be taken as an endorsement of the Treaty. However, a cursory glance at the newspapers of the day, and the assessment of almost all historians, is that the election of June

PEOPLE, POLITICS AND POWER

1922, imperfect and all as it was, did indeed represent a democratic endorsement of the Treaty.

Some of the most prominent anti-Treaty candidates lost their seats including Margaret Pearse, the mother of 1916 hero Padraig Pearse, Kathleen Clarke, the wife of Tom Clarke, and Countess Markievicz. Another implacable foe of the Treaty who lost out was Erskine Childers, who with just 512 votes was last of 10 candidates in the Kildare-Wicklow constituency. In Galway where there were eight candidates for seven seats the one to lose out was Liam Mellows, the leader of the 1916 Rising in the county.

Unfortunately, the election was not the end of the matter and the civil war began a few days after the votes were counted. The issue at stake in that war was whether the new Irish state would be a democracy or whether it would fall victim to violent self-appointed armed rulers as much of Europe had already done, or was to do in the decade that followed. Irish democracy was to prove far more resilient than either Irish republicans or a smug British establishment expected, but the price the country paid was extremely high.

COUNTESS MARKIEVICZ (1868–1927)

Countess Constance Markievicz was elected to parliament in 1918, in the first election in which women were allowed to stand and vote. She was one of two women elected to that Parliament, the other being the Conservative, Lady Astor. After her election she was appointed to the cabinet of the First Dáil as Minister for Labour.

Constance Gore-Booth was born into a wealthy land-owning family in Lissadell, County Sligo. She was presented to Queen Victoria in 1887 and took her place in society as a member of the landed gentry. Her ambition to be a painter took her to Paris where she met and ultimately married a young Ukrainian Polish land-owner, Casimir Markievicz, with similar artistic ambitions. Her family were so concerned about the attachment that they asked the British Government for information about Casimir. British and Russian intelligence agents compiled a dossier on him and it was sent back to Lissadell.

After periods living in Paris and the Ukraine the couple settled in Dublin in 1903 and Constance became involved in the Gaelic League and then with Sinn Féin. In 1909 she founded Fianna Éireann, an organisation designed to teach boys how to use weapons. Many of the young men who took part in the 1916 Rising came through the ranks of the Fianna. In 1913 she ran a soup kitchen during the Lockout and became involved in the Irish Citizen Army. Around this time Casimir left for the Ukraine and didn't return for over a decade.

Constance took a prominent part in the 1916 Rising and personally shot and killed a policeman. She was sentenced to death but had the sentence commuted. In 1917 she converted to Catholicism. After her election in 1918 she served two jail sentences for Sinn Féin activities. Constance was a strong opponent of the Treaty but lost her Dáil seat in the general election of June 1922. Jailed during the Civil War, Constance went on hunger strike with 92 other female prisoners; she was released after 30 days. She regained her seat in 1923 and was one of the founder members of Fianna Fáil in 1926. She was re-elected in June 1927, but died the following month. Casimir returned from the Ukraine to be at her death bed.

TOM KETTLE (1880–1916)

A politician, a poet, a teacher, a writer, Tom Kettle, was killed in the Battle of the Somme in September 1916. He was born in 1880, the 7th of 12 children of Andrew Kettle, a farmer and political activist who was one of the founders of the Land League and a strong supporter of Parnell. After O'Connell's Schools and Clongowes, Tom went on to UCD where he established himself as one of the leading figures of his generation. A brilliant scholar and a prominent student politician he was elected auditor of the Literary and Historical Society for 1898/99 and became good friends with other bright young men like James Joyce and Oliver St John Gogarty.

His political involvement began with the campaign against the Boer War. Although his progressive views on issues like women's rights and education were regarded as very advanced by the political establishment, he was chosen to run as the Irish Party candidate in 1906 in East Tyrone and was elected to the House of Commons at the age of 26. A contrast to the aging conservative males who dominated the Party, Kettle quickly became a national figure, although his popularity encouraged a fondness for drink that would become a problem. In 1909 he married Mary Sheehy, a fellow UCD graduate and suffragette, whose father was a well-known MP and whose sister, Hanna, married Frank Skeffington.

Appointed a professor at UCD in 1909 he was a hugely popular teacher. He had sympathy with the strikers of 1913 and wrote extensively about the appalling conditions of the Dublin poor. He joined the Volunteers in 1913 and was on a mission to Belgium to buy guns when war broke out in 1914. Kettle was horrified by the German atrocities he witnessed and wrote about them for the liberal *Daily News*. His passionate support for Belgium's cause prompted him to back Redmond's line on the war. Kettle joined the army remarking during one controversy: 'It is a confession to make and I make it. I care for liberty more than I care for Ireland.'

Because of his drinking Kettle was not dispatched to France until July 1916. The Rising caused him enormous grief, particularly as his brother-in-law, Frank Sheehy-Skeffington, was murdered by British soldiers. He came forward to give evidence in favour of his friend and UCD colleague, Eoin MacNeill, at his court martial.

Conditions in the trenches quickly ruined Kettle's health. He refused to take a safe staff job, preferring to stay with his men. He was killed on 9 September 1916, while taking part in the Irish Brigade's capture of Ginchy.

CHAPTER FOUR

THE FREE STATE

By the time the Dáil convened after independent Ireland's first general election, political life had been transformed by tragedy. The three giants of the Independence movement – Griffith, Collins and de Valera – were no longer available to lead the country. Both Griffith and Collins were dead and de Valera was in open revolt against the democratically elected Government. WT Cosgrave, known as a modest and unassuming Dublin city Councillor, was the man who was presented with the task of leading his country through the most difficult and critical phase of its history.

Between the election at the end of June 1922 and the first meeting of the Third Dáil in early September – the country had slipped over the precipice into civil war. Immediately after the election Collins issued an ultimatum to Republicans to vacate the Four Courts, one of many public buildings across the country, which they had occupied a few months earlier. When they refused, he ordered the Free State army to attack the building and after three days of fighting the garrison surrendered. Street fighting took place in Dublin and O'Connell Street was again left in ruins, only six years after 1916. In a major military offensive the Free State forces then drove the Republicans out of all the major towns by the end of August. After that the IRA took to guerrilla war.

Collins took leave from his position as chairman of the Provisional Government at the end of June to concentrate on winning the war and Cosgrave was elected by his colleagues as acting chairman of the Provisional Government in his place while Griffith continued on as President of Dáil Éireann. The first meeting of the third Dáil was postponed on a number of occasions during July and August because of the precarious military situation. The IRA threatened to kill Ministers so they were compelled to live together under military guard in the newly acquired Government buildings in Upper Merrion Street.

In August the Free State suffered two hammer blows. First, Griffith died of a stroke at the age of 51, worn out by work and worry. And 10 days later on 22 August came the news of Collins's death at Beal na Bláth. He was killed in an ambush by an IRA unit while he was travelling through his native West Cork. The cabinet met that night in Cosgrave's office and, almost by default, he was asked to assume the leadership. He decided immediately to summon the first meeting of the Third Dáil. When it met on 9 September, Cosgrave was proposed and elected as president of the executive council, as the cabinet was termed by the Treaty. The Republican TDs boycotted the Dáil but all other parties attended. The Third Dáil met in Leinster House, the former home of the Dukes of Leinster, which by then was the property of the Royal Dublin Society. Having moved between the Mansion House and Earlsfort Terrace Cosgrave decided it was time the Irish parliament settled down in a permanent home. The RDS had built an auditorium at Leinster House and the building was acquired by the state.

Unlike most Irish politicians of the day, Cosgrave had an aversion to long and flowery speeches. He used as few words as possible and had a dry sense of humour that infuriated opponents and heartened his supporters. On the day the Dáil first met at Leinster House *The Irish Times* published a perceptive profile of the unexpected leader:

> It would be hard to imagine anybody who is less true to what we used to consider the Sinn Féin type than Mr Cosgrave. It is not only that he does not dress in the regulation way – trench coat, leggings and slouch hat and the rest of it; but he has a thoroughly Conservative face. He is neither a wild-eyed revolutionary nor a lank-haired poet. He dresses generally in sombre hues, wears a bowler hat and looks rather like the general manager of a railway company.

This seemingly very ordinary man was required to do extraordinary things during his first few months as leader. During September 1922 the civil war intensified and the Government responded with an Emergency Powers Bill. This provided for the setting up of military tribunals empowered to impose the death penalty on anybody caught in possession of weapons. The executions began a month later when four young men found guilty of carrying illegal arms in Dublin were shot by a firing squad. A week later one of the republican leaders, Erskine Childers, was tried, convicted and executed in a similar fashion.

The response of the IRA was to escalate its campaign by listing 14 categories of people who were to be 'shot at sight'. This included all members of the Dáil who had voted in favour of the Emergency Powers Act. Republicans were also instructed to kill members of the Senate, High Court judges, journalists and proprietors of 'hostile newspapers' and 'aggressive Free State supporters.' There followed IRA attacks on politicians, journalists and ordinary citizens.

As the civil war escalated Cosgrave had to face other problems. A draft constitution had to be finalised and enacted. A police force was hurriedly established but it was an unarmed force in contrast to its predecessor the RIC. This was one of the most important moves Cosgrave made in legitimising the institutions of the new state. On 6 December, the first anniversary of the Treaty, the Dáil enacted the new constitution. The Irish Free State formally came into being and the provisional Government ceased to exist. Cosgrave was re-elected as President of the Executive Council of Dáil Éireann.

The day the constitution was enacted two Dáil deputies were shot in Dublin on their way to Leinster House. Sean Hales was killed and Padraic Ó Maille, the Leas Ceann Comhairle, was wounded. After the shooting some TDs fled Dublin in fear of their lives. Cosgrave believed that if the Dáil wilted in the face of terror then democracy could not survive. He ordered the secret service to go after the fleeing deputies and bring them back to Dublin. In reprisal the cabinet ordered the immediate execution of four imprisoned IRA leaders: Rory O'Connor, Liam Mellows, Richard Barrett and Joe McKelvey – one from each province. The next morning the four were executed at Mountjoy Jail. The country was shocked and there was outrage among Labour and other Opposition TDs but Cosgrave was unapologetic about the draconian response to IRA terror. 'There is only one way to meet it and that is to crush it and show them that terror will be struck into them,' he told the Dáil.

The other preoccupation of the Government was the enactment of a new constitution. In the spring of 1922 Collins tried to produce a document that could be accepted by republicans but the British were having none of it. They insisted on clauses enshrining the Oath and the status of the Governor General. Nonetheless, the constitution was a classic liberal democratic document. Under its terms all authority was derived from the people, the Oireachtas consisted of the Crown, represented by the Governor General, the Senate and the Dáil. Power was exercisable by an executive council, headed by a president, which was elected by and responsible to the Dáil. Voting was to be by proportional representation.

By the end of 1922 the constitution was in place and the civil war was effectively won but the violence continued to flare. On the night of 13 January 1923, Republicans burned down Cosgrave's home at Beechpark. The orgy of burning and destruction continued through the spring of 1923 but the IRA campaign gradually fizzled out. By April some 13,000 republicans had been interned in jails and camps throughout the country and de Valera sought to negotiate a truce. Cosgrave insisted on the following terms:

(a) That all political issues whether now existing or in the future arising shall be decided by the majority vote of the elected representatives of the people.

(b) As a corollary to (a) that the people are entitled to have all lethal weapons within the country in the effective custody or control of the Executive Government responsible to the people through their representatives.

The acceptance of these principles and practical compliance with (b) by the surrender of arms to be the preliminary condition for the release of prisoners who shall be required to subscribe to (a) and (b).

De Valera would not accept the terms but by this stage Republicans were in no position to bargain. On 24 May Aiken ordered the IRA to stop fighting and dump arms. De Valera issued a stirring message to the IRA hailing them as the 'Legion of the Rearguard' who had saved the nation's honour. The civil war was over.

Cosgrave and his Government had saved Irish democracy from being strangled at birth but at a terrible cost. The horror of the executions policy was compounded by the activities of death squads who met republican terror with counter terror. The actions of all sides in the civil war poisoned the political atmosphere for decades. Far more people died in the fratricidal strife than were killed in the War of Independence.

As well as the human cost, Cosgrave and his Government also faced the massive financial cost of reconstruction. The country's infrastructure had been systematically wrecked by republicans; in today's terms the damage was probably more than €10 billion. For a newly independent state without great financial resources the task of reconstruction was immense. Yet Cosgrave and his ministers were determined to rebuild the country without recourse to borrowing. They were particularly anxious not to go cap in hand to the British looking for financial assistance. They were also determined to put the nation's finances on a sound footing and did not fall into the temptation of printing more money for short-term popularity. The downside of that was that it entailed austerity and even suffering for a great many people.

In the absence of republicans, who refused to recognise the legitimacy of the Dáil, Cosgrave had a strong majority. While no formal party structure existed among his supporters they acted to all intents and purposes like a political party. The legitimacy of the Dáil was copper fastened by the fact that the Labour deputies, under the leadership of Tom Johnson, took their seats and became the official Opposition.

In January 1923, a convention of pro-Treaty government supporters took place in Dublin to discuss the formation of a party and in April 1923 Cumann na nGaedheal (the Party of the Gaels) was launched at a meeting in the Mansion House in Dublin.

When the Civil War formally ended in May Cosgrave decided to call a general election. Under the terms of the Constitution the Dáil was expanded from 122 members to 153 and all adults over the age of 21 were entitled to vote. The Irish Free State was one of the first countries in the world to give women the vote on the same basis as men. In the UK women had to wait until 1928, in France until the 1940s and in Switzerland until the 1970s.

The election was held in September 1923 and Cumann na nGaedheal emerged as the largest party with 39% of the vote and 63 seats. The anti-Treaty republicans, who had kept the name Sinn Féin, won 28% of the vote and 44 seats while Labour took 14 seats, the Farmers Party 15 and Independents 17. Cosgrave did not have an overall majority but, as Sinn Féin continued to boycott the Dáil, he had a comfortable majority. However, the total vote for parties who accepted the Treaty, at less than 70%, showed a significant slippage since the pact election of a little more than a year earlier.

In the Dáil Cosgrave was an effective speaker, as he had demonstrated during the Treaty debates, but he was not an orator. In cabinet he generally behaved as first among equals rather than as a charismatic leader. Brian Farrell in his definitive work: *Chairman or Chief* puts Cosgrave into the chairman category. His cabinet was full of brilliant intellectuals like Kevin O'Higgins, Paddy Hogan and Eoin MacNeill, the hard Northerner, Ernest Blythe, and the tough Minister for Defence, Richard Mulcahy.

The Government's tight fiscal policy came as a shock to a public hoping that Independence would lead to prosperity. Blythe, as Minister for Finance, went into political folklore for his decision to cut a shilling off the old-age pension in 1924 and to cut the salaries of teachers and other public servants by 10%. These cuts became a millstone around the Government's neck and, ironically, the very people whose civil war activities made the austere measures necessary were the ultimate political beneficiaries. Still, the Government had many positive things to its credit. The decision to build the electricity generating plant at Ardnacrusha and the establishment of the Local Appointments Commission to remove patronage from State appointments helped lay the new state on a firm foundation. Socially progressive legislation such as the control of rents and mortgages and the division of tens of thousands of acres of land under Patrick Hogan's Land Act of 1923 was also enacted.

Another early achievement was the establishment of a highly-respected diplomatic service. Cosgrave initially expressed scepticism as to whether a 'pampered' diplomatic service was really necessary but he quickly saw the need for it as a concrete expression of the Free State's independence among the nations of the world. The country joined the League of Nations and Cosgrave led the Government delegation to

Geneva in September 1923. On the home front the creation of an efficient and almost incorruptible civil service was a huge achievement. Almost all of the personnel had served in the British civil service and they brought their ethos and training into the service of the new state.

One of the features of Irish life after Independence was the increasingly Catholic nature of the Free State. Cosgrave was devout, even by the standards of his day. He attended Mass and Communion every day and, like a great many people in Ireland at the time, said the Rosary every night. He considered handing over the site of the GPO in Dublin for the building of a Catholic Cathedral as there was not one on any main street in Dublin as a result of a hangover from the penal laws. As President of the Executive Council he travelled to Rome on a number of occasions and his close friend, the far from pious, Oliver St John Gogarty, wrote facetiously that Cosgrave's 'piety greatly embarrassed His Holiness, the Pope.'

When the Attorney General, Hugh Kennedy, sought clarification as to whether divorce would continue to be allowed on the British model Cosgrave's response was swift. He introduced a bill in the Dáil banning divorce. 'I consider that the whole fabric of our social organisation is based upon the sanctity of the marriage bond and that anything that tends to weaken the binding efficacy of that bond to that extent strikes at the root of our social life,' he told the Dáil. The increasingly Catholic nature of the Free State caused concern to intellectuals like WB Yeats and it reinforced the Unionist claim that 'Home Rule would be Rome Rule'.

It was not the increasingly Catholic ethos of society but the economic austerity measures that caused the Government's popularity to slide. That drift was accelerated by other problems. In 1924 there was near mutiny in the Army over plans to prune its numbers. The Minister for Industry, Joe McGrath, resigned from the cabinet in protest. McGrath and other disillusioned Government backbenchers subsequently resigned from the Dáil in protest at the affair.

Another problem arose in late 1925 when the Boundary Commission, which had been expected by nationalist Ireland to remove two counties from Northern Ireland and hand them over to the South – ended in a fiasco. Instead it proposed that South Armagh and some other pockets of Northern territory should become part of the Free State but also that Protestant East Donegal should be handed over to Northern Ireland. Cosgrave did a hasty deal with the British to suppress the report and allow the existing boundary to stand. The deal also annulled the Council of Ireland provisions in the 1920 Government of Ireland Act. The Free State's financial obligations to the UK were cancelled in return. This abandonment of Northern nationalists was something that would have political consequences way into the future.

Meanwhile de Valera became increasingly frustrated at the inability of the anti-Government faction to capitalise on the Government's woes because of Sinn Féin's refusal to recognise the legitimacy of the Third Dáil. When de Valera failed to get the required majority to drop the principle of abstentionism at the Sinn Féin ard fheis in March 1926, he led his followers out of the party. On 16 May de Valera and his supporters launched a new party called Fianna Fáil (The Soldiers of Ireland) which still adhered to an abstentionist policy but only as a tactic. At that first meeting the party laid out its core principles as being the establishment of a 32-county Irish republic, the restoration of the Irish language, a social system to provide equality of opportunity, the distribution of land to the greatest number of people while making Ireland economically self-sufficient.

The name Fianna Fáil was picked quite deliberately for its mythical connotations. De Valera's chief lieutenant, Seán Lemass, wanted to call the new organisation simply 'The Republican Party', but his chief would have none of it. For de Valera the name echoed the golden age of Finn Mac Cumhail, it was also used in the first line of the chorus of the national anthem and, as Dev himself wryly observed, it was nearly impossible to translate.

De Valera got a chance to test the appeal of his new party a year later when Cosgrave called a general election in June 1927. The result came as a shock to Cumann na nGaedheal. The party's vote dropped by more than 10% and it won just 47 seats. Fianna Fáil in its first outing was close behind with 44 seats, leaving Sinn Féin with a rump of 5. Labour did well, winning 22 seats, the Farmers Party had 11, the Redmondite National League had 8 and there were 16 others. Cosgrave retained power only because Fianna Fáil and Sinn Féin TDs refused to enter the Dáil because of the Oath. De Valera led his TDs to Leinster House and demanded entrance to the Dáil without having to take the Oath. The doors were slammed in his face.

Then on 10 July came an outrage that transformed the political scene. The Minister for Justice, Kevin O'Higgins, widely regarded as the strongman of the Government, was gunned down on his way to Mass in the quiet Dublin suburb of Booterstown. Cosgrave responded with a tough, new Public

Safety Bill and, more significantly, with an Electoral Amendment Bill that required all Dáil candidates in future to take the Oath. This confronted de Valera with a critical dilemma: either Fianna Fáil accepted the oath or the party would not be in a position to contest the next election. De Valera responded by leading his party into the Dáil in August and accepting the Oath as an 'empty political formula' by signing their names in a book which had the Oath on the top of the page.

Fianna Fáil's entry to the Dáil left Cosgrave in a minority. De Valera made a deal with Labour leader, Tom Johnson, that Fianna Fáil would support a minority government led by Labour, if Cosgrave was removed from office.

Fianna Fáil and Labour were so confident of forcing Cosgrave out of office in August 1927, that they didn't even muster their full quota of TDs on the day of the confidence motion. One Labour TD, TJ O'Connell, was at a teachers' conference in Canada and didn't come home with the newspapers speculating that Cosgrave would lose by 73 votes to 69.

On the day of the debate the figures began to change as some Redmondite and Independent TDs began to have second thoughts about backing an unholy alliance of Fianna Fáil and Labour. The key to the vote turned out to be Alderman John Jinks, TD for Sligo. Jinks, a member of the National League Party led by John Redmond's son, Willie, was known to be unhappy at his leader's decision to bring down Cosgrave. Major Bryan Cooper, a former Unionist who now supported the Government, brought Jinks to Buswell's Hotel opposite the Dáil and plied the Sligo-man with drink. Jinks then disappeared from the precincts of Leinster House and mysteriously ended up on the Sligo train when the division was called in the Dáil. The vote was tied at 71 votes for each side and the Ceann Comhairle gave his casting vote in favour of the Government. Cosgrave had survived by the skin of his teeth, thanks to the disappearance of Jinks.

Soon afterwards Cosgrave dissolved the Dáil. The election of September 1927 saw Cumann na nGaedheal increase its strength from 47 to 62 seats but Fianna Fáil also increased from 44 to 57. Labour and the other smaller parties took a hammering and the two big parties were left to confront each other in the Dáil. Although they were under increasing pressure, in the Dáil and outside it, Cosgrave and his Ministers worked away doggedly in domestic affairs and with great success in international affairs. At the Imperial Conference of 1931 the brilliant Minister for External Affairs, Paddy McGilligan, broadened the scope of Irish independence by getting agreement to remove the remaining elements of subordination in the relationship between the UK and its Dominions. Known as the Statute of Westminster this enabled Dominion parliaments to pass legislation contrary to that passed at Westminster. It was regarded as a vindication of Collins's claim that the Treaty could be used as a stepping stone to greater freedom.

Meanwhile Fianna Fáil began to build its support base among the voters. Its economic programme was based on the principle of protectionism and the party focused its attacks on Agriculture Minister, Paddy Hogan, for his reforms aimed at making Irish agriculture competitive in a free trade environment. One of the issues Fianna Fáil focused on in particular was the land annuities which involved the payments made to the British Exchequer by Irish farmers, in return for the loans to buy out their land under the various Land Acts. The issue represented a combination of nationalist rhetoric and economic self-interest as far as farmers were concerned.

Fianna Fáil also played the Catholic card quite ruthlessly. Despite his personal piety Cosgrave was not personally sectarian. He faithfully stood by the clause in the Treaty to appoint representatives of Southern Unionism to the Senate. Fianna Fáil attacked him furiously for this and accused him of being involved in a 'Masonic plot' with Protestant members of the Senate.

Fianna Fáil also attacked him for allowing 'immoral publications' to circulate in Ireland and demanded even more rigorous censorship than that in operation.

The infamous Dunbar-Harrison case illustrates how religion could be used as a political football. In 1930 the Local Appointments Commission appointed a Protestant, Letitia Dunbar-Harrison, to the vacant position of Mayo County Librarian. The County Council refused to ratify the appointment on the grounds she did not speak Irish but nobody was in any doubt that the reason was that she was a Protestant. The Government responded by dissolving the County Council and appointing a Commissioner in its place who duly appointed Miss Dunbar-Harrison to the post.

The reaction from Fianna Fáil was one of outrage. De Valera maintained that if the functions of the appointee were merely those of an attendant handing out books then religious affiliation would not matter. 'On the other hand, if the whole idea behind the scheme was that the librarian should go into the homes of people, and into the schools, and push the scheme, if instead of her duties being passive they were active, the position was an entirely different one.'

With his political opponents playing a discreet sectarian tune Cosgrave also came under pressure from Archbishop Gilmartin of Tuam but he wrote to the prelate as follows: 'As I explained to Your Grace at our interview, to discriminate against any citizen – or exercise a preference for a citizen – on account of religious belief would be to conflict with some of the fundamental principles on which this state is founded.' Cosgrave eventually opted for a political fudge and Dunbar-Harrison was transferred from Castlebar to the Department of Defence library in Dublin and a Catholic librarian installed in her place.

As the 1930s dawned the Cumann na nGaedheal Government appeared obsessed with defending the Treaty settlement of a decade earlier. In response to sporadic outrage and murder by the IRA the Government introduced the draconian Public Safety Acts of 1927 and 1931 and the Jurors' Protection Act of 1931. These gave the Government sweeping powers and allowed military tribunals to try terrorist offences. Fianna Fáil and the Labour Party denounced the measures in the Dáil, and while Cosgrave and his Ministers vigorously defended their approach the electorate grew increasingly weary of the security emphasis.

By contrast with the Government, Fianna Fáil put the Civil War behind it, but retained most of its republican support through studied ambiguity. In 1928 Seán Lemass famously described Fianna Fáil as 'a slightly constitutional party'. On the other hand, Fianna Fáil cleverly added practical policies, based on voter self interest, to its intrinsic republican appeal. For farmers it was the abolition of the land annuities, for the urban working class it was the promise of jobs through industrial development and for business it was the promise of protective trade barriers.

Even the style of dress adopted by Ministers served to alienate them from the voters. The wearing of formal morning suits, wing collars and top hats was the normal dress code for people of their position at the time but it gave the Government a remote air. The Wall Street Crash and the world economic recession that followed in the early 1930s put the Cosgrave Government under even more pressure and an increasingly confident and well-organised Fianna Fáil was convinced its hour was at hand.

SIR MAURICE E. DOCKRELL (1850–1929)

Sir Maurice E. Dockrell performed the notable feat of being the last Unionist elected in the South in the general election of 1918. From a prominent Protestant merchant family in Dublin, Maurice kept the Unionist flag flying in the capital during the Parnellite era. He was beaten in the general election of 1885 by William Martin Murphy in a contest for the St Patrick's Division. He had better luck standing out against the Sinn Féin tide in 1918, when he was elected for the Rathmines Division.

His son Henry M. Dockrell (1880-1955) was also a prominent politician. He was one of a deputation of Southern Unionists who negotiated with de Valera before the Truce of 1921. He entered politics in 1932 standing for Cumann na nGaedheal and was elected to the Dáil on his first outing. He remained a TD until 1948.

Henry's two sons in turn became long-serving TDs. Maurice Dockrell (1908-1986) was elected as a TD in 1943 and served in the Dáil for the next 34 years. He lost his seat in the Fianna Fáil landslide of 1977. He was Lord Mayor of Dublin in 1960/61. His brother, Percy Dockrell, was a TD for Dún Laoghaire from 1951 to 1977. Like his brother, he too lost out in 1977. Asked why he thought he had lost his seat he is said to have remarked. 'Liam (Cosgrave) didn't get enough votes for me.' Percy Dockrell had been consistently elected on the Cosgrave surplus.

Dockrell's was one of the landmark stores in Dublin until it was burned to the ground in a malicious fire in the 1970s.

ALFIE BYRNE (1882–1956)

Known as 'the shaking hand of Dublin', Alfie Byrne was one of the most popular politicians ever to emerge from the city. Elected to the House of Commons as an Irish Party MP at a by-election for the Harbour Division of Dublin in 1915 he was ousted by Phil Shanahan of Sinn Féin in 1918. Four years later he returned to national politics in the first-ever democratic election held in independent Ireland in June of 1922, comfortably winning a seat in Dublin Mid Division as an Independent.

Alfie was elected in Dublin North in 1923, polling over 10,000 first preferences, and was re-elected as an Independent at every subsequent election until 1954. He consistently racked up enormous majorities, his biggest ever being in 1932 when he won over 18,000 first preference votes, well over two quotas. He was Lord Mayor of Dublin from 1930 to 1939 and had another stint in the Mansion House in 1954/1955. Two of his sons were elected as TDs in the 1950s.

One of the stories about Alfie during his stint as Lord Mayor involved the film star Mae West. The world famous star, who coined the phrase 'come up and see me some time', met Alfie at a function during a visit to Dublin and tried out the line on him.

'Ah, I'm afraid I won't be able to come up and see you,' responded   the Lord Mayor.

'Why not?' said Mae with mock indignation.

'It's Lent,' replied a smiling Alfie.

'Then come up and see me when you get it back,' she retorted.

CHAPTER FIVE

THE AGE OF DE VALERA

The moment de Valera had been waiting for came in January 1932, when Cosgrave called a general election. It marked one of the critical turning points of twentieth century Irish politics. Just five years after its foundation Fianna Fáil was ready for office. Cumann na nGaedheal had been in power for ten difficult years and while Cosgrave and his Government had done a remarkable job in laying the foundations of a democratic state, the voters wanted change. Fianna Fáil put forward a series of optimistic policies that matched the public mood and contrasted with the continuing austerity promised by the government. The party had also developed a superb organisation and had the open support of the IRA, which added a bit of muscle to intimidate opponents.

De Valera had a keen sense of theatre, which he deployed to good effect in the election campaign. His routine was to arrive quietly at major provincial centres well in advance of the advertised time for a Fianna Fáil public meeting. He would then go to the edge of town where his supporters would have a horse waiting for him, preferably a white one. De Valera, dressed in his trademark, a long black cape, would mount the horse and proceed into town flanked by a band of horsemen with blazing sods of turf held aloft on pitchforks. The electrifying effect of this entrance to a drab Irish provincial town on a dark winter evening can only be imagined.

By contrast with the colour and organisation of the Fianna Fáil campaign, Cumann na nGaedheal looked rather dull. The party relied on the support of local notables rather than developing a strong organisation. It did come up with some inspired negative propaganda but that was not enough to make up for the deficiencies in organisation and policies. 'The Shadow of a Gunman – Keep it from your Door,' read one anti-Fianna Fáil election poster while a newspaper advertisement read: 'The gunmen are voting, the Communists are voting Fianna Fáil.'

The most famous Cumann na nGaedheal poster of all read: Devvy's Circus, absolutely the greatest road show in Ireland today – Señor de Valera, world famous illusionist, oath swallower and escapologist. See his renowned act: Escaping from the straitjacket of the republic. Frank F. Aiken, fearsome fire-eater. Shaunty O'Kelly, the man in dress clothes. Monsieur Lemass, famous tight rope performer, see him cross from the Treaty to the Republic every night. Performing frogs, champion croakers, marvellous trained sheep.

The election campaign was bitter and even violent at times. Cumann na nGaedheal speakers had difficulty getting a hearing as the campaign got increasingly disruptive with the IRA coming out to support the Fianna Fáil campaign. Government speakers were shouted down with opponents demanding: 'Who started the civil war?' and 'Who ordered the execution of Rory O'Connor?' A standard Cumann na nGaedheal reply to such hecklers was: 'And how many banks did you rob?' At Cosgrave's final election rally at College Green in Dublin passions boiled over as rival supporters fought each other on the streets and the gardaí had difficulty in quelling the riot. 'There were cheers and counter cheers, scuffles took place among the crowds, free fights developed and batons were drawn,' reported the *Irish Independent.*

The rowdy scenes did nothing to halt the bandwagon. Even the Catholic Church, which had excommunicated de Valera and his followers during the Civil War, quickly established good relations with the party. Some of the bishops and many parish priests continued to support Cosgrave but the curates tended to support Fianna Fáil. De Valera even had backers among the hierarchy and at senior levels in Rome. Leading Fianna Fáil TD, Sean MacEntee, boasted after the election that Fianna Fáil had won the Catholic vote.

When the election took place on 16 February the voters opted for change. Fianna Fáil increased its share of the vote from 35% to over 45% while Cumann na nGaedheal slipped from 39% to 35%. In terms of seats de Valera had 72 while Cosgrave won 57. It was a shattering blow to Cosgrave and Cumann na nGaedheal to lose an election to the forces they had defeated in the civil war, ten years earlier, but a younger electorate was looking to the future, not the past.

Still, with 72 seats out of 153, de Valera was 5 seats short of an overall majority and he needed outside support to form a government. When the Seventh Dáil met on 9 March de Valera was elected as President of the Executive Council with the backing of the Labour Party, which had done badly in the election dropping from 13 seats to 7. More surprisingly de Valera was supported by three Independents including, James Dillon, son of the last leader of the Irish Party.

It was a tense first day with rumours sweeping Dublin that the Cosgrave Government would refuse to hand over power to their Civil War opponents. An army coup was widely talked about. De Valera's son, Vivion, carried a revolver in his pocket as he accompanied his father into the Dáil. A number of senior Fianna Fáil TDs were also armed as they entered the Dáil chamber. Frank Aiken handed out revolvers to some of his colleagues and rumour had it that even heavier weapons were on hand in case of an army coup. James Dillon claimed in later years that he saw a senior Fianna Fáil politician assembling a machine gun in a telephone booth at the back of the chamber.

While some wild men on the Government side had talked about a coup, particularly the garda commissioner, Eoin O'Duffy, there was no widespread sympathy for such a move in Cumann na nGaedheal and Cosgrave was not prepared to countenance it. He asked colleagues where the rumours were coming from and was told about O'Duffy, whom he had never liked or trusted in the first place. Before the critical vote, far from being engaged in any frantic plotting, Cosgrave was upstairs in his room playing pontoon with the former Education Minister, John Marcus O'Sullivan. Cosgrave's acceptance of the election result and the calm manner in which he handed over power to de Valera was as important for the future of Irish democracy as his victory over anti-democratic forces in the Civil War.

On taking office de Valera immediately slashed the salaries of TDs and Ministers so that politicians would earn the same kind of salaries as ordinary citizens. It was a hugely popular move that cemented the image of Fianna Fáil as the party of working people. Another popular decision was de Valera's refusal to wear a top hat and frock coat on formal occasions, as Cosgrave and his Ministers had done. Such populist touches endeared him to ordinary voters. He also looked after his republican allies by releasing all IRA prisoners. The IRA had decoupled itself from Sinn Féin in the 1920s and at this stage was in an informal alliance with Fianna Fáil.

On the political front de Valera quickly began to implement his party manifesto by abolishing the Oath and refusing to pay the land annuities to the British Exchequer. The British responded with the imposition of punitive tariffs on Irish exports, mainly cattle and agricultural produce. This had a ruinous effect on the Irish economy, particularly the farming community. In the long run it was politically beneficial for Fianna Fáil because the hardship being imposed from Britain generated heightened nationalist sentiment.

Speaking at the first party ard fheis after the election de Valera delivered a speech that encapsulated his party's appeal. Summoning up the dead generations and focusing on the near mystical aspiration of a united Irish republic, as well as on the practical programme of Government he said: 'It may not be given to us in our time to see the end, but the young faces that I see here are pledged to the day when the work so many died to accomplish will pass into good hands if we fail.' The emphasis on the unattainable national ideal gave Dev a powerful weapon to motivate his party over the decades that followed.

As 1932 wore on de Valera became worried about his ability to govern without a secure Dáil majority. When it came to the national finances Fianna Fáil turned out to be as conservative as Cumann na nGaedheal and that led to tension with the Labour Party. A new round of wage cuts across the public service was mooted but Labour made it clear it would not countenance such a move. On the law and order front, the establishment of the Army Comrades Association, as the Cumann na nGaedheal response to the IRA, threatened street disorder of the kind that was happening in other European countries, particularly Germany. There was also unrest in rural Ireland. Following the Government's decision to withhold the land annuities from the British exchequer, most farmers simply stopped paying. De Valera wanted them to continue the payments to the Irish Government but the farmers were having none of it, particularly the large farmers who had supported Cosgrave.

At the end of 1932 de Valera decided on a snap general election that confounded his opponents and startled his supporters. In the course of a short campaign he promised Irish farmers that he would halve the land annuities if the Government got a new mandate. The election, in January 1933, was a triumph for de Valera. He won a clear overall majority with 77 seats and almost 50% of the vote. Cumann na nGaedheal declined again and Labour received its lowest share of the popular vote in the history of the state. A new farmers' movement called the Centre Party won 11 seats and an array of Independents was also elected. De Valera was able to dispense with the Labour Party and run the country on his own terms.

Conflict with Britain on the one hand, and his old Civil War enemies on the other, helped de Valera reinforce his power base among small farmers and urban workers. He sacked the Garda Commissioner, Eoin O'Duffy, who took over as leader of the Army Comrades Association. The Association changed its name to the National Guard and began to adopt some of the trappings of the fascist movements then popular in continental Europe, the most striking being the blue shirt. Shirted political movements had a long history going back to Garibaldi's Redshirts, who had spearheaded the unification of Italy in the 1860s. However, by the 1930s in the shape of Hitler's Brownshirts and Mussolini's Blackshirts they represented profoundly anti-democratic forces. The adoption of the blue shirt by the National Guard, who not surprisingly became known as the Blueshirts, threatened to bring sinister European style fascism into Irish politics.

Shortly after O'Duffy took over as leader of the Blueshirts in the summer of 1933, he staged a confrontation with de Valera's government by announcing a march on Dublin by units from around the country. De Valera banned the march and the Blueshirt threat fizzled out. The movement ceased to be a threat to the democratic Government but it continued on as nationwide movement, drawing supporters from different anti-Fianna Fáil groups.

In late 1933 the Blueshirts came together with Cumann na nGaedheal and the Centre Party to form a new party called Fine Gael (Family of the Gael). O'Duffy became the party leader, although he did not have a seat in the Dáil, while Cosgrave was the leader in Leinster House. O'Duffy's extremism and political inexperience quickly undermined his standing as party leader and he was forced to step down as Fine Gael leader in 1934 with Cosgrave taking over the position. His movement continued to exist in various guises until 1936 when he left Ireland with some of his supporters to fight on the side of Franco in the Spanish Civil War.

The Blueshirt episode has always been something of an embarrassment to Fine Gael. While the formation of the ACA was quite understandable, given the level of IRA intimidation in the early 1930s, the drift to a fascist-style movement by some of the people most closely associated with the establishment of the democratic institutions of the state was something they never lived down. It took Fine Gael a long time to recover from O'Duffy's involvement and it was a contributing factor in ensuring that the party would always struggle to match Fianna Fáil.

With its political opponents in disarray Fianna Fáil pursued protectionist policies during the 1930s and tried, with limited success, to develop a native manufacturing base behind tariff walls. The Economic War with Britain, resulting from de Valera's efforts to dismantle the Treaty, entrenched Fianna Fáil as the dominant political force in the country. In the new conflict with Britain, de Valera managed to forge a common identity between his party and the nation while making his critics appear anti-national. With an overall majority in the Dáil, he was able to pursue the holy grail of unfettered national sovereignty based on his Document Number Two. Ironically, he was able to do this on the basis of the looser form of Dominion status the Free State Government had achieved in the Statute of Westminster.

Fianna Fáil's continuing strength was based on the combination of nationalist rhetoric and policies aimed at improving the lot of working people and, while those policies did not always succeed, they reinforced Fianna Fáil's image as the peoples' party. The new industrial jobs which emerged behind the shelter of protectionism, big slum clearance projects and the building of new local authority housing schemes, the establishment of semi-state companies like Bórd na Móna, all combined to reinforce the party's power base. In

1932 the party's heartland was the west of Ireland with its small farms, but during the decade it managed to expand that base into all the big urban centres including Dublin.

The framing of a new constitution became a priority for de Valera in the mid 1930s. He had already introduced a number of amendments to the Free State constitution, which unlike its successor could be amended without a referendum. Having already abolished the Oath in 1932, he eliminated references to the King and the Governor General from the Constitution in 1936, following the abdication of King Edward VIII. He also abolished the Seanad, a long target for Fianna Fáil because it gave significant representation to the Protestant minority.

De Valera, though, hankered after a constitution of his own to put his own indelible stamp on the country he governed. The constitution was drafted by a small team of civil servants working under his supervision. He also consulted academic, legal and religious authorities, including John Charles McQuaid, principal of Dev's alma mater, Blackrock College, and the rising ideologue of an increasingly confident Catholic Church.

The main features of the 1922 constitution in relation to the powers and operations of the executive, the Dáil and the courts were retained but there were some very important additions. Article 2 defined the national territory as the whole island of Ireland, although Article 3 limited its jurisdiction to the 26 counties. Articles 12 to 14 provided for the election of a President at head of state while the Senate was reconstituted as a vocational body elected by local politicians. Article 34 gave the Supreme Court power to review the constitutionality of new legislation while Articles

Above: Delegation on its way to open negotiations with British Prime Minister Lloyd George in 1921. L to R: Arthur Griffith, founder of Sinn Féin; Robert Barton, signatory of the Treaty; Larry O'Neill, Lord Mayor of Dublin; Count Plunkett, first Sinn Féin MP, elected in Roscommon 1917; Eamon de Valera.
Below: Harry Boland, Michael Collins and Eamon de Valera, 1919.

Left: WT Cosgrave as leader of the Opposition addressing an Army recruitment meeting in 1939.

Right: Captain's Prize Day at Milltown Golf Club, April 1955. An Taoiseach, John A. Costello teeing off the first tee watched by from left: JD Kearns (Hon Sec), John Tummey (captain), Comdt P. Downs (Sec) and representative Price, who played with the Taoiseach.

Above: Seán Lemass with Willy Brandt, Mayor of West Berlin.

Below: Eamon de Valera kisses the ring of papal nuncio Monsignor Roncalli. Behind are, left to right: Monsignor Lommel, coadjutor Archbishop of Luxembourg; Sean Mac Bride, Irish foreign minister; Monsignor McQuaid, and Taoiseach John A. Costello. Luxeuil, France, 22 July 1950.

Above: 1916 Exhibition, 12 April 1966. John A. Costello looking at the greatcoat worn by Mic Collins at the historical exhibition in the National Museum, Kildare Street, Dublin.

Below: Anglo-Irish lunch in London, 18 March 1963. Prime Minister Harold Macmillan and Taoiseach Seán Lemass, with Frank Aiken, Minster for External Affairs.

Right: William Norton, Labour
Party leader from 1932 to 1960.

Left: Charles Haughey,
Neil Blaney and Captain
James Kelly during the
Arms Trial, 28 May 1970.

Above: Brendan Corish, leader of the Labour Party from 1960 to 1977, campaigning in front of the Labour slogan of the sixties. Michael O'Leary in the far-right corner.

Below: Outside 10 Downing Street, 24 November 1972. Prime Minister Edward Heath shakes hands with Taoiseach Jack Lynch.

Above: Former Taoiseach, Jack Lynch, in his office on his last day in Dáil Eireann, 1981.

Below: Charles Haughey speaking at the unveiling of an eight-foot statue of Eamon de Valera outside the courthouse in Ennis, County Clare, 1981.

Left: Garret FitzGerald and Charles Haughey, 1982.

Right: February 1992. A furious Charles Haughey, post phone tapping allegations (end of January 1992).

40 to 45 reflected the influence of Catholic social thinking with a strong emphasis on fundamental rights concerning the family, education, private property and religion.

At the time the aspect of the constitution that generated most controversy was the role of the President. The Opposition mistakenly believed that de Valera intended it to become a semi-dictatorial office occupied by himself. The special position accorded to the Catholic Church in Article 44 was also a bone of contention, then and later, while there were protests by some republicans that Article 3 represented an acceptance of partition.

De Valera held a referendum on his new constitution on the same day as the general election in July 1937. The Irish people passed the constitution, but the victory margin of 54% to 46% was hardly resounding. The general election result was even less emphatic with the Fianna Fáil vote slipping almost 5% to 45% and leaving the party without an absolute majority in the Dáil. The party won 69 seats in a smaller Dáil of 138 deputies. The reduction came about because of a constituency revision designed to maximise the number of Fianna Fáil seats, which involved the abolition of the two university constituencies of NUI and TCD. Fine Gael polled a respectable 35% and won 48 seats, while Labour recovered from the disaster of 1933 by winning over 10% of the vote and won 13 seats. There were eight Independents.

De Valera was unhappy at the failure to win an overall majority and within 11 months he dissolved the Dáil and went to the country again. As in 1933, the tactic paid off with Fianna Fáil winning 77 seats and pushing its share of the vote up to 51.9% – the highest it has ever achieved in the history of the state! Fine Gael and Labour both lost ground and de Valera was back with a clear overall majority. His timing was carefully calculated. Through 1937 and the early months of 1938 he had been negotiating with the British to end the Economic War and a deal was struck in April of 1938. The crucial aspect of the deal as far as de Valera was concerned was that the Treaty ports were handed over by the British to Irish jurisdiction. This was to prove of vital importance during the Second World War. De Valera tried to raise the issue of partition but was firmly rebuffed by the British who made it clear they would not discuss the issue without the agreement of the Northern Ireland administration. Craig refused to countenance any change in the status quo on partition and the matter was dropped from the talks. Once it was out of the way the two Governments came to an amicable agreement. The British dropped their tariffs on Irish goods and in return were given preferential treatment in Ireland. A lump sum of £10 million was accepted in settlement of the land annuities and – most importantly of all in the light of what was to come – the Treaty ports were handed over to the jurisdiction of the Irish Government. Although the deal was a compromise it was not portrayed as such and marked a political triumph for de Valera. The voters showed their approval by giving him his greatest-ever electoral triumph in 1938.

With a secure majority in the Dáil and his constitution in place de Valera was at the height of his power at the end of 1938, but the world was moving towards war. Ireland had played a full role at the League of Nations in the 1930s. De Valera was a supporter of the notion of collective security as an alternative to the system of alliances led by the great powers, but the rise of Hitler and Mussolini now made the League irrelevant. The outbreak of the Second World War in September 1939 was a cataclysmic event that led to the deaths of tens of millions of people across the globe in the years that followed. Ireland was sheltered from the full impact of the war, because of its geographical location, but it still presented the Irish Government with a dilemma.

De Valera was determined to adopt a neutral stance, as a further assertion of sovereignty. It was a pragmatic response to the outbreak of world war and it also served to paper over a number of political cracks. There was no serious internal opposition to the policy of neutrality between the forces of fascist dictatorship and those of democracy. James Dillon was the only prominent politician to oppose it and he left Fine Gael to be free to express his views on the issue.

The most immediate security threat at the beginning of the war came not from outside the country but from Sinn Féin and the IRA who allied themselves with the Nazi war effort. Having released IRA men from jail in 1932 de Valera turned on the organisation a few years later once the Blueshirt threat was out of the way. When the IRA began a bombing campaign in Britain in 1939 de Valera feared the country's neutrality might be compromised and he moved to crush the organisation. The Offences Against the State Act of 1939 gave the Government sweeping powers to deal with subversives and they used those powers including internment without trial, military tribunals and the death penalty to defeat the IRA. Over the next 5 years 16 IRA men were hanged or shot after trial by military tribunals with de Valera proving himself every bit as ruthless as Cosgrave in his dealings with republicans.

PEOPLE, POLITICS AND POWER

After the fall of France in June 1940, Winston Churchill presented de Valera with a dilemma. The new British Prime Minister asked Ireland to join the Allies and offered a united Ireland in return. The offer was turned down on the basis that the British might not be able to deliver a united Ireland without Unionist consent. It was an ironic stance given that before and since Irish Government policy has been that the British had it in their power to compel Unionists to agree to a united Ireland. In the summer of 1940 another consideration was also paramount: de Valera's Government believed that the Germans were going to win the war.

De Valera continued to adhere to neutrality even after the US entered the war against the Nazis in 1942. The Americans were far less understanding than the British about the reasons for neutrality and relations between de Valera and the Roosevelt administration were extremely frosty. As war raged across the world Ireland became detached from international events. During what became known as 'the Emergency' draconian censorship kept most Irish people largely ignorant of what was happening outside their shores.

Isolated from the catastrophe sweeping most of the globe time seemed to stand still in de Valera's Ireland. In a famous St Patrick's Day radio broadcast in 1943 he outlined his view of the good life.

> That Ireland which we have dreamed of would be the home of a people who valued material wealth only as the basis of right living, of a people who were satisfied with the frugal comforts and devoted their leisure to the things of the spirit – a land whose countryside would be bright with cosy homesteads, whose fields and villages would be joyous with

the sounds of industry, with the romping of sturdy children, the contests of athletic youth and the laughter of comely maidens, whose firesides would be the forums for the wisdom of serene old age. It would, in a word, be the home of a people living the life that God desires that a man should live.

The Irish people found de Valera's vision attractive at an ideal level but it did not work in practice. While enough people supported him to keep him in office, emigration began to turn to a flood again in the 1940s as tens of thousands of young people rejected the notion of frugal comfort and fled the country for England to work in the war industries or join the Allied forces in the fight against fascism. Politically neutrality paid off for de Valera. He called an election for June 1943 and Fianna Fáil returned to power for the fifth time in a row. However, he was back with a minority government as the Fianna Fáil share of the vote dropped 10% compared to 1938. Luckily for Fianna Fáil the Fine Gael share of the vote dropped by even more and the beneficiaries were Labour and a new farmers party called Clann na Talmhan (Family of the Land).

Although Labour had one of its best ever elections, winning almost 16% of the vote and 17 seats it was unable to capitalise on the achievement because of a vicious row that split the party. The row had its origins in the readmission of Jim Larkin and his son, Jim Jnr, to the party in 1941. Both Larkins were nominated as official Labour candidates in Dublin in 1943 despite the strenuous objections of William O'Brien, the ITGWU boss, and both were elected. In January 1944 the ITGWU disaffiliated from the party on the grounds of 'communist infiltration'; eight Labour TDs were members of the union and five of them left the party to establish National Labour, under the leadership of James Everett.

The fragmented opposition allowed Fianna Fáil to remain in office but de Valera waited for the right moment to do what he had done twice before. After a Dáil defeat he made another run to the hustings in May 1944. Just as in 1933 and 1938 the electorate rewarded his gamble by giving him another thumping majority with 76 seats out of 138. Fine Gael dropped to 30, the 2 Labour parties lost 5 between them with official Labour winning 8 and National Labour 4. Clann na Talmhan lost 2 seats to end up with 11.

At the end of the War de Valera did untold damage to Ireland's international reputation by making a bizarre visit to the German legation in Dublin in May 1945 to pay his condolences on the death of Hitler.

He also traded insults with Churchill after the British Prime Minister had attacked Irish neutrality. De Valera's supporters were delighted – but these incidents only served to highlight Ireland's apparent indifference as to whether the dark forces of Nazism or those of western democracy had triumphed in the War. De Valera performed extraordinary political feats in pursuit of sovereignty but, as Europe was rebuilt after the War, Ireland remained cut off as an impoverished backwater.

JIM LARKIN (1876–1947)

The iconic figure of the Irish Labour movement, Larkin founded the two unions that merged into SIPTU long after his death. Charismatic, colourful and filled with energy, Larkin transformed the lives of Irish working-class people, yet he was also a deeply divisive figure whose actions did serious damage to the movement that he played such a part in creating.

Larkin was born in Liverpool to Irish parents. He worked on the docks and became a militant socialist and union activist. His career as a unionist organiser began in Belfast but it was in Dublin that he founded his own organisation, the ITGWU, in 1909, to cater for unskilled workers like dockers, carters and labourers who lived in dreadful conditions in the slums of the city. Larkin also established a newspaper, *The Irish Worker,* as an alternative to the mainstream press.

He helped found the Irish Labour Party in 1912 along with James Connolly, but it was his involvement in the great lockout of 1913 that made him a national figure. It was a bitter eight-month dispute that the workers eventually lost. Still, the ITGWU survived but did not expand until after the Rising, when it was reorganised by William O'Brien after the execution of Connolly.

Disillusioned and depressed, Larkin went to the US to raise funds in 1914 and after the outbreak of the WWI he stayed there. Involved in the American Communist Party, he was arrested during the red scare of 1920 and sentenced to ten years in prison. He was released in 1923 as an act of clemency by the Irish American governor of New York, Al Smith.

Larkin returned to a hero's welcome in Ireland but a bitter rift developed in the ITGWU with William O'Brien who, in Larkin's absence, had built it from a union with 5000 members to one with almost 100,000. After a bitter dispute Larkin left to join the WUI, founded by his brother Peter, and the row spilled over into the Labour Party. Larkin and his supporters established the Irish Workers' League which fielded candidates in the election of 1923 and did some damage to the Labour Party. The League was pro-communist and pro Soviet Union and it failed to make any serious impact – but it did damage Labour. Larkin went to Moscow in 1924 and was elected to the Comintern executive, which promoted the cause of Soviet communism across the world.

In September 1927 Larkin was elected to Dáil Éireann as an Independent Labour candidate, but he was unseated as an undischarged bankrupt. His financial problems arose from his loss of a libel action he took against William O'Brien. He was elected to the Dáil again in 1937 and this time was able to take his seat. However, he lost it in 1938. In 1941, he and his son, Jim Jnr, joined the Labour party and he was elected again in 1943 but lost his seat again in 1944. The involvement of the two Larkins in Labour prompted a split in the party with the withdrawal of the ITGWU faction that formed National Labour. Big Jim Larkin died in 1947. The two Labour parties united in 1950, but it was not until 1990 that the ITGWU and the WUI merged as SIPTU.

TOM JOHNSON (1872–1963)

The first parliamentary leader of the Labour Party, Tom Johnson, is one of the unsung heroes of Irish political history. Born in Liverpool, he left school at the age of 12 to become a messenger boy. At 19 he got a job with an Irish fish merchant and spent half the year in Liverpool and the other half at the Irish fishing ports of Dunmore East and Kinsale. In 1900 he got a job as a commercial traveller based in Belfast; where his connection with trade union activity began. Johnson's enthusiasm helped him rise rapidly through the union ranks and he became vice president of the ITUC in 1913 and then president in 1916.

Anxious at all times to preserve the unity of the Irish Labour movement – Johnson was not a supporter of the Rising of 1916. He was the joint secretary of the Mansion House conference that organised the nationwide anti-conscription movement and he helped organise the anti-conscription strike of 1918. He was also a member of the small group that drafted the Democratic Programme of the First Dáil.

Johnson showed great courage in 1922 in defying both Collins and de Valera and insisting on the right of the Labour Party to contest the election called in June of that year. Despite massive intimidation by republicans, Labour contested 18 constituencies and won 17 seats. The party's stance helped to ensure that the people were given a democratic choice rather than being forced to accept the Collins-de Valera pact.

Johnson led the Labour Party into the Dáil and provided the main opposition to the Free State Government until Fianna Fáil took its seats in August 1927. A fierce critic of the executions policy, adopted by the Cosgrave Government; Johnson's role as leader of the opposition helped to legitimise the Dáil in the eyes of most voters after the Civil War. He came within a whisker of becoming the head of government in 1927, after Fianna Fáil entered the Dáil and promised to back a Labour-led Government. The plan failed because a number of TDs, including Labour's TJ O'Connell, were absent for the vital vote of confidence in the Cosgrave government. Johnson lost the election called immediately afterwards in September 1927. The intervention of James Larkin Jnr in his County Dublin constituency contributed to the loss. Johnson served in the Seanad until 1936.

CHAPTER SIX

THE ERA OF INTER-PARTY GOVERNMENTS

The mood in the country began to change after the Second World War. As a shattered Europe was rebuilt Ireland's economy continued to languish and living standards actually fell. National teachers went on strike in 1946 and after a long and bitter dispute were forced into abject surrender by the Government. The mood of resentment among teachers, who had long been regarded as pro-Fianna Fáil, further undermined the Government's popularity. Then in 1947 a new political party, with a strong appeal to disaffected Fianna Fáil supporters, arrived on the scene.

Clann na Poblachta (Family of the Republic), led by Sean MacBride, one of the most exotic figures in Irish political history, made an immediate impact. MacBride, a son of the celebrated Maud Gonne, was one of the country's leading barristers in the 1940s although in his younger years he had been an active IRA man and was chief of staff in the 1930s. His legal father was John MacBride, one of the executed 1916 leaders, but his biological father was a radical French politician and throughout his life Sean spoke with a noticeable French accent. The new party appealed to the more radical republican wing of Fianna Fáil and to younger voters looking for change. Fianna Fáil had moved to the centre over its 16 years in office, following strictly orthodox economic policies, and adopting the kind of draconian law and order measures to deal with republican violence that it had resolutely opposed during the

1920s. This approach left the door open for a challenge on its republican flank. As well as focusing on partition Clann na Poblachta also adopted a left-wing stance on social issues that threatened Fianna Fáil's working-class base.

Clann na Poblachta contested three by-elections in October 1947, and sensationally won two of them. MacBride was elected in Dublin County and Patrick Kinnane was elected in Tipperary. De Valera decided that the best way to deal with the threat to Fianna Fáil hegemony was to nip it in the bud. He dissolved the Dáil 18 months before he needed to and called an election for February 1948.

The election campaign was widely portrayed in the media as a contest between the tired and aging Fianna Fáil, which had been in power continuously for 16 years, and the vibrant new Clann. Fine Gael was widely written off as a spent force, as the party fielded fewer candidates than Clann na Poblachta and almost half its sitting TDs did not even contest the election.

Labour was still divided and, while the death of 'Big Jim' Larkin in 1947, took a lot of venom out of the split, the two Labour parties remained deeply suspicious of each other.

IClann na Talmhan was also pushed to the sidelines in the publicity stakes by the newcomer. Clann na Poblachta campaigned vigorously denouncing Fianna Fáil not only for its lack of imagination but for alleged corruption. The Clann fielded the second largest number of candidates after Fianna Fáil and there were huge expectations that it would be the second largest party in the new Dáil.

In the event de Valera's election gamble largely paid off, but not quite in the way he hoped. Fianna Fáil won almost

42% of the vote and 67 seats in the 147-member Dáil. An Ioverconfident Clann polled a disappointing 13% but the yield in seats was even worse at just 10, far lower than its proportion of the vote should have delivered. Too many candidates, poor tactics and overconfidence contributed to the disappointing result for MacBride's party. Fine Gael defied the prophets of doom – not for the last time – by holding on as the second party in the state with 31 seats on just 19% of the vote. Labour won 14 seats and National Labour got 5, Clann na Talmhan won 7 and there were 12 Independents. The breakaway Congress of Irish Unions, dominated by the ITGWU, made strenuous efforts to persuade the four National Labour TDs to support the election of de Valera as Taoiseach. There was considerable confidence in Fianna Fáil that the party would be back for another term as a minority Government.

In the immediate aftermath of the election it was still widely anticipated that Fianna Fáil would come back to power with the support of the anti-communist National Labour and some of the Independents. De Valera fully expected to resume where he left off. However, the Fine Gael leader, Dick Mulcahy, who had succeeded WT Cosgrave as leader of Fine Gael in 1943, set about putting an alternative Government in place. Initially it seemed an impossible task as it did not appear that the pro-Commonwealth Fine Gael could work with the ultra-republican Clann na Poblachta, the two rowing Labour parties and Clann na Talmhan.

In the event, the desperation among all the Opposition parties to put de Valera out of office led to a deal. Mulcahy had to make a big personal sacrifice in order to get an agreement. Republicans of the Clann, especially MacBride viewed Mulcahy as an unacceptable Taoiseach – they had not forgotten that he presided over the executions of 77 anti-Treaty prisoners. Mulcahy agreed to stand aside in favour of his Fine Gael colleague, John A. Costello, who became the first Taoiseach of an Irish coalition Government. The impact of the change is vividly captured in an anecdote told by Patrick Lindsay, then a Fine Gael barrister from Mayo, who was later to serve in cabinet. On the day the Dáil choose the new Taoiseach, Lindsay had to drive from Mayo to Galway to see a client.

> I drove into Tuam and I saw there the large physique of a man, a civic guard, who was standing on the footpath. I pulled in diagonally and lowered my window.
> 'Guard is there any news from Dublin?'
> 'At ten past five this afternoon Mr John Aloysius Costello was elected Taoiseach of this country.'
> I knew by the way he said it that this really meant something to him and I said:
> 'Guard would you like a drink.'
> 'We'll have two.'
> 'Will you wait a minute until I park this car?'
> 'Leave it where it is. We have freedom for the first time in 16 years.'
> We had more than one drink that day.

Costello is now virtually the unknown Taoiseach, although he served two terms in office. A Dubliner, he was born in 1891 and was educated by the Christian Brothers at O'Connell School and then at UCD. He subsequently qualified as a barrister and, while he did not participate in 1916 or the War of Independence, he was appointed Attorney General in 1926 and represented the Free State Government at the League of Nations and at Imperial Conferences. Elected to the Dáil in 1933, Costello was not regarded as a prominent politician in 1948 although he was a leading lawyer. He emerged as Taoiseach largely because he was the most acceptable Fine Gael politician to MacBride. Costello and MacBride shared membership of that most exclusive club, the Law Library, which was more important in many ways than party affiliation. Costello was also popular with Labour because he had represented the union movement in a number of important court cases.

The task of making what was in effect a six-legged coalition work was enormous. Not only were there five distinct parties, but the Independents were also represented at cabinet by James Dillon, who became a successful Minister for Agriculture. Fine Gael had six cabinet posts with its two leading Ministers, Patrick McGilligan at Finance and Mulcahy at Education – the only members of the Government with Ministerial experience. Clann na Poblachta and Labour got two seats each while National Labour and Clann na Talmhan got one, and Dillon represented the Independents. MacBride took over at Foreign Affairs and a relatively unknown young colleague of his, Noël Browne, was given the Health portfolio. Browne, a medical doctor, was intense, idealistic, confident and possessed of a flair for publicity that nobody else in the Government could match.

The Inter-Party Government, as it became known, was not expected to last a year but it lasted more than three. It has gone down in history for the spectacular manner of its collapse, but it actually had a number of achievements to its credit and it showed that coalition Governments could work. Keynesian economic policies were adopted and the Exchequer purse strings loosened. Houses were built, social welfare increased, the health service expanded, poorer farmers catered for and money spent in disadvantaged areas on ambitious schemes like afforestation. A more outward looking trade policy and initiatives like the creation of the Industrial Development Authority (IDA) by the Minister for Industry and Commerce, Dan Morrissey, were the first crucial steps in the slow transformation of Ireland from a desperately poor economy, based on subsistence farming, to a more affluent one, based on international trade.

Yet for all its successes the first Inter-Party Government is remembered mainly for two controversial episodes: the declaration of the Irish Republic, and The Mother and Child Scheme.

De Valera had avoided declaring the Irish Republic for fear it would copper fasten partition. MacBride, though, was determined that the final step to full Irish independence should be taken and Costello was happy to oblige, despite resistance from the pro-Commonwealth element of Fine Gael. The niceties of external association were lost on most people and there was a popular mood to complete the road to full independence for the 26 counties by repealing de Valera's External Relations Act and declaring a Republic. What caused controversy was the manner in which the announcement was made by the Taoiseach during an official visit to Canada. Although the matter had been discussed and agreed in principle at cabinet, the decision had not been formally ratified or communicated to the British. While Costello was in Canada, the *Sunday Independent* newspaper in Dublin reported that the External Relations Act was about to be repealed. Costello was asked about this at a press conference in Ottawa and he astonished everybody by telling the truth and confirming that his Government did indeed intend to repeal the Act. He then went a step further and confirmed that it was also the intention to declare a Republic.

The secretary of the Department of Foreign Affairs, Freddy Boland, felt the announcement had been made 'in a burst of indiscretion' and reported that all he could say in response to the flood of phone calls to his office was that 'our Prime Minister has simply made an awful gaffe.' He went on to remark: 'Jack Costello had about as much notion of diplomacy as I have of astrology ... You can safely say that if de Valera had remained in power we would have remained in the Commonwealth but all references to the Crown etc. would have been eliminated from the Act.'

While the decision was a popular one with the electorate it had negative implications for Anglo-Irish and North-South relations. The Government could actually have repealed the Act without leaving the Commonwealth as newly independent India was just in the process of signing up for membership, even though it was a republic.

The decision to leave served to reinforce partition. The response of the British Labour Government was the Republic of Ireland Act of 1949, which was primarily designed to reassure Northern Unionists about their status within the UK. The Act also provided that the Republic would not be regarded as a foreign country under British law, which enabled Irish citizens to retain the freedom to travel and settle in the UK without restriction.

In relation to the North, the Act specified that there could be no change in the status of Northern Ireland without the consent of its Parliament. Northern Ireland was a one-party state ruled by the Unionist Party. The nature of the partition settlement guaranteed the party a permanent majority that resulted in a very unhealthy democracy. The first election to the Northern parliament in 1921 saw 40 Unionists, 6 Nationalists and 6 Sinn Féiners elected. Just to secure Unionist hegemony proportional representation was abolished soon afterwards. The Nationalist Party was the last survival of the old Parliamentary Party with politicians like Joe Devlin still carrying the Parnellite flag. The 1920s and 1930s were a deeply depressing time for Northern Nationalists – they were excluded from power or any influence and subject to endemic discrimination. The failure of the Boundary Commission to change the border was a shattering blow but the anti-partition rhetoric of Southern politicians did nothing to help their cause. By convention the British Government let the Northern Government get on with its own business and its affairs were never debated in the House of Commons. Led by James Craig, the chief organiser of Unionist resistance to Home Rule in the Northern parliament, which met in the specially built and imposing surroundings of Stormont, was 'a Protestant Parliament for a Protestant people.'

After the Second World War the social spending

programmes of the British welfare state were extended to Northern Ireland and there was a gradual improvement in conditions for all citizens, although Catholics naturally resented their continual exclusion from political power. The declaration of the Republic by Costello and de Valera's simultaneous anti-partition campaign had the effect of reinforcing Unionist power.

In Britain, Clement Attlee's Labour Government, which had won a landslide victory over Churchill's Conservatives in 1945, was initially well disposed towards rectifying the discrimination against Catholics but, faced with an aggressive anti-partition campaign from the South, the Attlee Government backed the Unionists. Unionist support for the Allied cause in the Second World War, in contrast to the neutrality of the South, also served to promote sympathy for the Unionist position.

If the declaration of the Republic copper fastened partition, the other major controversy in the life of the Inter-Party Government demonstrated the power and authority of the Catholic Church and appeared to confirm the worst fears of Protestant Ulster that Home Rule had indeed resulted in Rome Rule. The Mother and Child Scheme of 1950 has gone down in Irish political history as the ultimate Church-State confrontation, with the Catholic Church demonstrating its power to dictate Government policy. The full story is far more complicated, but the conventional image does illustrate the larger truth that, just as Northern Ireland had evolved into a Protestant state, the Republic was a Catholic state by 1951. Tolerance was not a feature of political or social life on either side of the Border.

The Mother and Child Scheme was the brainchild of Noël

Browne, who was made a cabinet Minister on his very first day in the Dáil – at MacBride's insistence. As Minister for Health he achieved great success in the drive against tuberculosis, which had grown to epidemic proportions in the lean 1930s and 1940s. The discovery of antibiotics underpinned the campaign but Browne, whose own family had been devastated by the disease, will be remembered for eradicating the curse of TB.

He followed up that successful campaign with his Mother and Child Scheme. Briefly stated it was designed to provide free ante- and post-natal care for all mothers and free medical care for all children up to the age of 16. The Catholic hierarchy opposed it on the basis that the absence of a means test marked an unacceptable level of State intervention in medicine. In the autumn of 1950 Browne consulted the bishops and concluded that they would not oppose his scheme. His fatal move, though, was that in March 1951 he announced the scheme without Cabinet approval. The bishops objected and Browne and his Cabinet colleagues then agreed to abide by the hierarchy's judgement on whether the scheme was compatible with Catholic morality. The bishops said no, the Cabinet agreed to drop the scheme and Browne was asked to resign by his own party leader Sean MacBride. While the controversy has come to be regarded as a clash between Church and State a leading authority on the period, Professor Ronan Fanning, believes that 'the decisive breach was between Government colleagues rather than between Government and the hierarchy.' Neither was the affair an attempt to prevent poor women and children receiving free medical treatment – as is often thought. It was rich women and children the Church and

Irish Medical Association wanted excluded from the scheme. However, leaving all the political complications aside, the critical fact was that the Government allowed the Catholic hierarchy to determine what was acceptable public policy. It was the high point of Church power and a low point for Irish democracy.

The successes of the Inter-Party Government were overshadowed by the controversy. The Government fell shortly afterwards, although not because of Noël Browne's scheme. It collapsed because two Independents decided to withdraw their support over the price of milk. It was the hostility of the farmers to James Dillon, rather than the hostility of the hierarchy to Noël Browne that brought the formal end to the first Inter-Party Government.

When the election came in June 1951 Costello lost power but his party's fortunes revived. The Fine Gael vote rose by 6% from its all-time low in 1948 and the party gained nine extra seats. It was back in business as the main alternative to Fianna Fáil. The big loser was Clann na Poblachta which was reduced to two seats, with MacBride barely scraping election. Noël Browne ran as an Independent and was easily elected in Dublin South East. Clann na Talmhan's vote held up and the party won 6 seats while the Labour Party, which reunited in 1950, held its share of the vote but dropped 3 seats to 16.

Fianna Fáil was back in power but, with 69 seats in a 147 member Dáil, it was well short of an overall majority. Browne and a number of other former Clann members, who had been elected as Independents, voted for de Valera's nomination as Taoiseach and ensured that he regained office. Browne subsequently joined Fianna Fáil. The new Minister for Health,

Jim Ryan, did implement a modified version of the Mother and Child Scheme, which passed without contention, as it contained a means test acceptable to the Catholic Church. Apart from that the Government did not have any new ideas and reverted to the stale policies of the 1940s. Historian, Joe Lee, rates the 1951 to 1954 administration as the worst Government headed by de Valera. Austerity measures were pursued by the Minister for Finance, Sean MacEntee, and the glimmer of hope raised by the Inter-Party Government that better times might be on the way appeared to be eradicated. The Independents withdrew their support in the spring of 1954 and de Valera had no choice but to go to the country.

In the election of 1954 Fianna Fáil lost seats while the revival of Fine Gael continued. Costello was in a position to form his second Inter-Party Government although it was only composed of three parties this time around: Fine Gael, a reunited Labour and Clann na nTalmhan. Costello offered to include Clann na Poblachta, which had made a mini-comeback with three seats, but MacBride preferred to remain out of office although he supported Costello in the vote for Taoiseach. Economic stagnation continued although further seeds of economic recovery were sown by the Minister for Finance, Gerry Sweetman. His appointment of the brilliant young civil servant Ken Whitaker as secretary of the Department of Finance, over the heads of more senior colleagues, was one of the most significant actions of the second Costello Government. Another was the introduction of a zero corporation tax regime for profits earned on exports. The Government set out an outline for a programme of economic expansion and social reform. These initiatives were to have enormous consequences in later decades but in the mid 1950s there was no sign of a lift in the depression as Sweetman continued to impose the tight fiscal discipline that had characterised the previous Fianna Fáil administration.

The mood was summed up in an *Irish Times* editorial on the fortieth anniversary of the Rising in 1956 when the preliminary census figures showed the population had declined to 2.8 million: 'If the trend disclosed continues unchecked Ireland will die – not in the remote unpredictable future, but quite soon,' it said.

The second Costello Government also ran into trouble over an unexpected event, a renewed outbreak of IRA violence. The IRA's border campaign, launched in 1956, led to the deaths of RUC and IRA men. Costello responded in January 1957 by promising that the full resources of the Irish state would be used to prevent further cross-border raids. That prompted MacBride to announce that his party was withdrawing its support from the Government. Rather than face certain defeat on a motion of no confidence Costello dissolved the Dáil and called an election for March 1957.

The result was a decisive win for Fianna Fáil. De Valera returned to power again, 25 years after his first period in office. With 78 seats Fianna Fáil had a comfortable overall majority. Fine Gael and Labour lost seats while Clann na Poblachta was reduced to one – with MacBride losing his own seat. Sinn Féin made a significant breakthrough on the back of the IRA campaign, winning four Dáil seats but its TDs continued to adhere to the old policy of abstentionism and stayed away. The return of de Valera, who spent much of the election campaign justifying his stance on the Oath in 1926 rather than focusing on the country's endemic economic problems, did not auger well for the country's future. At the age of 75 he was back at the helm yet again. Young people were gripped by a mood of despair as emigration rose to astonishing levels. With Britain and most of the Western world basking in a period of economic boom, some Irish people even began to wonder if independence had actually been a big mistake. It was independent Ireland's darkest hour but, although nobody knew it at the time, the dawn was not far off.

WILLIAM NORTON (1900–1963)

Leader of the Labour Party for almost 30 years, Bill Norton, was one of the dominant political figures of his era and was twice Tánaiste and a senior Minister in the Inter-Party Governments. Unfairly pilloried in Noël Browne's autobiography, Norton's achievement was to keep traditional rural Labour and the urban radicals together most of the time. Although the party split in the 1940s – Norton managed to bring the two sides back together in 1950.

Born in Dublin he went to work for the Post Office in 1916. In later life he was subject to a campaign of vilification by Sean MacEntee of Fianna Fáil who accused him of wearing the uniform of the crown. The only uniform he ever wore was that of a post office messenger, which of course carried the insignia of the crown before 1922.

He became a union activist in his early 20s and became the full-time secretary of the Post Office Workers Union in 1924. He was elected as a Labour TD for County Dublin at a by-election in 1926 but lost the seat in 1927. Elected for Kildare in 1932 he held the seat at every election up to 1961. He became leader of the Labour Party immediately on his election as his predecessor, TJ O'Connell, lost his seat in 1932. Norton encouraged his party to put de Valera into office but was disappointed at Fianna Fáil's policies.

In 1943, he stood over the decision of the Dublin organisation to nominate Jim Larkin Snr and Jnr, even though he was personally opposed to their left wing pro-Moscow line. The result was that five ITGWU backed party TDs left the party to form National Labour. The two Labour parties joined the first Inter-Party Government in 1948 and Norton became Tánaiste and Minister for Social Welfare, introducing major reforms of the welfare code. He was Minister for Industry and Commerce in the second Inter-Party Government of 1954-1957. Norton stepped down as party leader in 1960 and Labour embarked on a more left-wing course for the following decade.

The longest-serving party leader in independent Ireland after de Valera, Norton's most notable feat was the introduction of compulsory social insurance. He also promoted a system of conciliation and arbitration in the public service that survived for more than half a century. Although more prosaic than Browne's Mother and Child Scheme, Norton's achievements proved more substantial.

MICHAEL DONNELLAN (1900–1964) AND JOSEPH BLOWICK (1903–1970)

The leaders of Clann na Talmhan (Family of the Land), the most successful small party in Irish political history until the foundation of the Progressive Democrats. The party won 14 seats in its first election and twice served in Government but disappeared completely from the political map, leaving hardly a trace. Clann na Talmhan which was founded in 1938 in Athenry, County Galway by Michael Donnellan with the aim of providing a voice to the small farmers of Ireland. Other key policy objectives were reduced taxes on farmers and a national programme of intensive afforestation.

In its first election in 1943 the Clann won 14 seats, mainly in the West and South but that number dropped to 11 in 1944. Donnellan was extremely disappointed by the loss of three seats – and resigned as leader. He was replaced by Blowick who had been elected in Mayo South as a Farmers Party TD in 1943 but switched to the Clann shortly afterwards.

In 1948 the number of seats won by Clann na Talmhan dropped again to seven but the party participated in the first Inter-Party Government with Blowick becoming Minister for Lands, and Donnellan Parliamentary Secretary at the Office of Public Works. They occupied the same posts in the second Costello Government. Their biggest achievements were investment in land drainage and a major programme of afforestation. The party's vote continued to decline and by 1961 only Blowick and Donnellan were left. When Donnellan died in 1964 his son, John, like his father the captain of an All-Ireland winning Galway team, was invited to contest the resulting by-election for Fine Gael and was elected. Blowick didn't run in 1965 and the party died. John Donnellan subsequently became Minister of State in the Department of Health from 1982 to 1987.

CHAPTER SEVEN

LEMASS LEADS ON

De Valera finally decided to call it a day as Fianna Fáil leader and Taoiseach in the early summer of 1959. To the relief of his cabinet he decided to quit in order to run for the presidency. He was succeeded as Taoiseach, without a contest, by Seán Lemass, a pragmatic, hard-headed politician, who had been his deputy leader for over 14 years. Lemass and de Valera were like chalk and cheese and it was an open secret in Fianna Fáil that the Tánaiste was becoming increasingly impatient at the reluctance of the Chief to hand over the reins of power. However, there was never a hint of this in public.

Although he was 60 when he became leader, Lemass threw off the shackles that had held Ireland back for so long and embarked on a range of imaginative economic, social and diplomatic policies that transformed the country in a few short years. Immediately after taking office Lemass made it clear that his priority would be bread and butter issues, rather than partition. During his relatively brief period in office Ireland joined the real world of international politics and took the first steps towards joining the European Community. National sovereignty ceased to be an issue.

A Dubliner, Lemass fought in the GPO in 1916, while still a schoolboy. He took part in the War of Independence and the Civil War and acquired the reputation of being a 'hard man'. A founder member of Fianna Fáil he always preferred to focus on practical problems rather than the abstractions favoured by de Valera.

Appointed Minister for Industry and Commerce in 1932 he served in that position in every Fianna Fáil Government until he became Taoiseach. As a Minister Lemass presided over the policy of protectionism and built his Department into a powerful empire. By the time he became Taoiseach, however, he knew that protectionism was no answer to the country's problems and he set out to dismantle it as quickly as possible.

The pipe-smoking Lemass had a passion for horse racing and poker. This encouraged rumours that he had a gambling problem, but as far as voters were concerned it was further proof of his human qualities. In contrast to many of his successors he did not believe in spending long hours in the Taoiseach's office and only canvassed at election time. He believed it was important to have time for reflection and be abreast of developments in economics and international relations, and he spent many evenings at his home reading.

On taking office Lemass formed a bond with the brilliant secretary of the Department of Finance, TK Whitaker. While the two did not always see eye to eye, as Whitaker was more economically orthodox than his Taoiseach, the combination of talents helped to transform Ireland.

Even before Lemass had taken office Whitaker, with the backing of his Minister for Finance, Jim Ryan, had drafted an economic recovery plan called the Programme for Economic Expansion that involved a substantial injection of state capital into productive enterprises over a five-year period. Implemented under Lemass the Programme stimulated the private sector into action and the annual rate of economic growth more than doubled to 4% in the early 1960s. The other major initiative taken by Lemass in his early years in office was to stop talking about partition on the international stage and to get involved in the United Nations with an independent stance on a range of international issues. He followed that up in 1961 by applying for membership of what was then called the European Economic Community (EEC) after the British had applied to join.

Lemass decided to go to the country in the autumn of 1961 in search of a mandate for his policies. By that stage the two main opposition parties also had new leaders. James Dillon, the son of the last leader of the Irish Party, and probably the most flamboyant orator in the history of the Dáil, succeeded Mulcahy as leader of Fine Gael. Dillion appealed to traditional Fine Gael supporters, particularly in rural Ireland, but had difficulty winning over voters in Dublin. Labour also got a new leader with Bill Norton stepping down after almost 30 years at the helm. He was succeeded by the earnest but capable Brendan Corish who embarked on a go it alone policy for Labour, announcing he would not enter a coalition. It was the beginning of Labour's move to the left during the 1960s when the party's slogan became 'The Seventies will be Socialist'. Corish's father was elected as a TD for Wexford in 1921 and the seat had been in the family since then. That long Labour pedigree gave Corish the credibility to set the party on a new course.

Lemass dissolved the Dáil in September 1961, and sought a mandate for the liberal economic policy that was just beginning to take effect. Despite the new-found optimism in the country Lemass barely scraped back to power. He only held on to the Taoiseach's office because the Opposition refused to offer the voters an alternative Government. The Fianna Fáil share of the vote dropped by just over 4% compared to 1957 and the party lost eight seats. Fine Gael and Labour both gained seats and between them had the same share of the vote as Fianna Fáil. However, the absence of a transfer pact cost them dearly and Lemass was in a position to form a minority Government supported by a handful of Independents.

In his second term Lemass built on his early achievements. Although many people expected him to try de Valera's trick of a snap election to obtain an overall majority, he was content to exercise power as long as the Independents supported him. A key element in his economic strategy was to build good relations with the trade union leaders. National wage agreements became a feature of economic planning and the bond forged with the union leadership was continued by successive Fianna Fáil administrations for the next 40 years, despite the formal link between the unions and the Labour party.

Lemass spurred economic growth and industrial development by dismantling trade barriers and developing foreign trade. In 1965 he signed the Anglo-Irish Free Trade Agreement which opened the huge British market for Irish exporters but also allowed cheap British imports into Ireland. Many in Fianna Fáil were unhappy at the way in which Lemass moved to develop Ireland into an industrial trading nation, abandoning the arcadian notion of an agricultural economy with the small farmer at its heart.

It was not only Fianna Fáil traditionalists who recoiled at the new direction. Denouncing the Anglo-Irish Free Trade Agreement Labour's Tipperary TD, Sean Treacy, claimed Lemass had 'perpetrated an act of union with Britain more final, binding and irrevocable than the Charter of Henry II or the Act of Union.'

Those who found the economic policy difficult to accept were even more appalled by Lemass's decision in January 1965, to visit Northern Ireland and meet the reforming Northern premier, Captain Terence O'Neill. Preparations for the first ever visit of an Irish head of Government to talk to his Northern counterpart took place in secret and hardliners, North and South, were taken aback when Lemass appeared at Stormont. The Lemass initiative marked the abandonment of sterile anti-partitionism and some of his supporters never got over the shock. In the North the welcome for the Taoiseach heralded the arrival on the political scene of an obscure preacher known as the Rev. Ian Paisley. During Lemass's second visit to the North Paisley hurled snowballs at the Taoiseach's car and spent the next 40 years throwing bigger and bigger metaphorical snowballs at every attempted rapprochement between North and South until he finally mellowed somewhat in 2006, at the age of 80, and agreed in theory to share power with Sinn Féin.

By the mid 1960s Lemass had transformed the economy and with it the image of Fianna Fáil. His achievement in keeping disciplined party unity, while effectively ditching most of the de Valera heritage as rapidly as he could, was a remarkable political achievement. He turned Fianna Fáil into a pragmatic party, committed to economic progress and good relations with Britain, while retaining its earlier image as a party of austere nationalist principle committed to the Irish Ireland vision of the 1916 leaders.

'Since 1959 Mr Lemass has worked wonders with this

material, (FF)' wrote the Trinity College political scientist, David Thornley, who was later to be a Labour TD. 'He has cemented the loyalties while refurbishing the image. Thirty years ago this was a party of republicanism, language revival, economic protectionism; today it is a party of realism, talks with Captain O'Neill, growth, planning, free trade.'

In line with his policy of opening doors Lemass brought in a whole new team of new Ministers. De Valera had brought in some new talent in 1957 with Jack Lynch, Neil Blaney and Kevin Boland coming in to replace some of the founding fathers in Government. Lemass prompted Paddy Hillery to fill the cabinet vacancy created by his own promotion in 1959 but it was not until his election victory in 1961 that he made substantial changes. He brought in George Colley, Brian Lenihan, Donogh O'Malley, and his son-in-law Charles Haughey. It was a brash new team in tune with the brash new times.

In March 1965, Lemass dissolved the Dáil 18 months early to capitalise on the enormous goodwill generated by the visit to the North. The Opposition was still divided with Labour continuing to reject coalition and campaigning on an independent strategy. This time Lemass pushed the Fianna Fáil vote up 4% to almost 48%, but won just two extra seats. Still with exactly half of the membership of the 144 member Dáil he was in a comfortable position to form a new Government. Fine Gael and Labour, between them, actually outpolled Fianna Fáil but in the absence of a coalition deal the extra votes did not translate into a majority of seats. Fine Gael won 47 seats on 34% of the vote while Labour won over 15% and pushed its seats total to 22. Failing for the second time to gain office James Dillon resigned as Fine Gael leader and was replaced by Liam Cosgrave, the shrewd but taciturn son of WT Cosgrave. Liam Cosgrave had done well as Minister for Foreign Affairs in the 1954-1957 Government but the brighter sparks in Fine Gael doubted his ability to win a general election.

Back in office, Lemass continued to promote new talent. Frank Aiken at Foreign Affairs was the only survivor of the 1926 front bench to remain in cabinet. Lemass then stunned the country in October 1966, by announcing his retirement from office just as his policies were coming into their own. The manner of his going precipitated a leadership struggle that was to have a profoundly divisive effect on Fianna Fáil for the next 30 years. The main contenders for office, in the eyes of the media, were two younger cabinet Ministers, Charles Haughey and George Colley, both aged 41, who were as different as chalk and cheese. Haughey, who was married to Lemass's daughter, was widely regarded as the representative of the brash new Ireland, his hands in various financial pies, impatient to escape from the stuffiness of de Valera's vision. By contrast Colley, the son of a party elder, was regarded as a clean-cut, Irish-speaking, representative of old values, re-packaged for the modern age. At the heart of the power struggle was not just a battle for supremacy between the men but a struggle for the soul of Fianna Fáil.

In the event that battle was put on hold because it threatened to wreck the party. Lemass intervened to ask a more conciliatory figure to put his name forward for the leadership. The apparently reticent compromise candidate was Jack Lynch, the Minister for Finance. Lynch should have been an

Above: Taoisigh Dr Garrett FitzGerald, Jack Lynch and Liam Cosgrave listen to Charles Haughey's speech, 19 January 1990.

Below: Charles Haughey surrounded by a crowd outside Leinster House during the leadership wave of 1983.

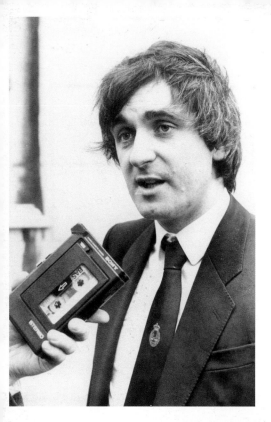

Left: Bertie Ahern, Fianna Fáil Chief Whip in the 1980s.

Below: Conor Lenihan, Bertie Ahern and Brian Lenihan during the presidential campaign of 1990.

Above: Alan Dukes, Fine Gael leader and Dessie O'Malley, Progressive Democrats leader, announcing FG-PG electoral pact, 6 June 1989.

Right: Dessie O'Malley and Mary Harney shortly after the foundation of the PDs.

Right: The Minister for Finance, John Bruton, entering Leinster House. Budget, July 1981.

Below: At the exhibition of modern Irish trade union banners in the Project Gallery, Dublin. From left: the Fianna Fáil leader, Charles Haughey, Ger O'Leary, Francis Devine, Irish Labour History Society and the Minister for Labour, Ruairi Quinn, 1986.

Left: Dick Spring and Albert Reynolds leaving the negotiations room at the Berkeley Court Hotel during the discussions which led to the formation of a coalition government in 1993.

Below: Albert Reynolds and Mary Robinson, 1993.

Above: Adrian Hardiman, Michael McDowell and Liz O'Donnell, 7 June 1987.

Below: Albert Reynolds, Joe Walsh, Charles Haughey and Bertie Ahern outside the Mansion House.

Left: Gerry Adams, Albert Reynolds and John Hume outside Government Buildings after the 1994 IRA ceasefire.

Right: The Fine Gael leader, John Bruton and James Nugent, SC arriving at the Beef Tribunal in Dublin Castle, 22 June 1992.

Above: New Fianna Fáil leader, Bertie Ahern with his daughters, Cecilia (13) and Georgina (1
20 November 1994.

Below: Green Party TDs Eamon Ryan, John Gormley, Trevor Sargent, Paul Gogerty, Dan Boy
and Ciaran Cuffe protesting against failed Government policies, 25 January 2006.

obvious candidate for the leadership from the beginning but his claims were obscured by the media speculation about the Haughey-Colley rivalry and by his own reluctance to seek the position. Not only did Lynch occupy the most important Ministry but he was a national sporting hero, due to his exploits as a hurler and footballer in the 1940s when he won six All-Ireland medals in a row: five for hurling and one for football. It is a record that has never been equalled in the history of the GAA.

Lynch was born in Shandon in Cork city in 1917, the fifth of seven children of a quiet hard-working tailor, Dan Lynch and his wife Norah. Lynch's political background was different to that of most members of the cabinet. His family did not come from the republican tradition but from old style Cork politics. Lynch's father was a supporter of William O'Brien and the political stories he was told as a child concerned O'Brien's struggle against the Redmondites to control Cork politics. Elected to the Dáil in 1948, Lynch impressed de Valera and rose rapidly in the ranks, being appointed to the cabinet as Minister for Education in 1957. Lemass promoted him to Industry and Commerce in 1959 and to Finance after the 1965 election. When Lemass asked him to stand for the leadership Lynch agreed after some persuasion and Haughey and Blaney withdrew from the contest. Colley, however, pushed it to a vote and Lynch won easily by 51 votes to 19.

The new Taoiseach was widely regarded as an interim leader who would, after a few years, hand over to one of his more charismatic Ministers. He promoted Haughey to Finance and retained all the other Ministers in his cabinet. He was pushed into a decision in 1968 to hold a referendum to try and change the voting system from multi-seat PR (STV) to the straight vote. The difficulty of winning an overall majority in the Dáil under PR had rankled with Fianna Fáil for some time. De Valera made an attempt to change the voting system in 1959 but the voters rejected the initiative in a constitutional referendum on the same day that they elected him President. Lynch was pushed by some of his more aggressive colleagues like Kevin Boland, into an ill judged second attempt to get rid of PR in 1968. The voters again rejected Fianna Fáil's attempt to change the voting system and Lynch's authority suffered a knock.

When he went to the country in June 1969 there was a widespread feeling in the media that it was time for change. In tandem with the country's new-found prosperity close links had developed between Fianna Fáil and the business community. This was epitomised by an organisation called Taca which attracted enormous publicity in the 1960s. It was a fund-raising organisation of 500 businessmen who attended monthly dinners in the Gresham Hotel and were given special access to Ministers in return for contributions to the party. Haughey and his group, including Donogh O'Malley and Lenihan, were prominent attenders of Taca dinners but so were traditionalists like Blaney and Boland who defended the organisation to the hilt.

Haughey was the politician most associated with Taca in the public mind as he organised the first dinner, a lavish affair attended by the whole cabinet. 'We were all organised by Haughey and sent to different tables around the room,' Kevin Boland recalled. 'The extraordinary thing about my table was that everybody at it was in some way or other connected with the construction industry.' The love affair between Fianna Fáil and the construction industry was one that was destined to last.

Opposition TDs questioned the whole ethos of the organisation and, in particular, the links between Ministers and property developers. There were suggestions about the selection of property being rented by Government Departments and State agencies that were mushrooming at a time of unprecedented economic growth. In particular there were persistent rumours about a link between Haughey and John Byrne, one of the first property developers on the scene, who built O'Connell Bridge House which was promptly leased by the Government.

Opposition TDs questioned the propriety of the cosy relationship between Fianna Fáil and the building industry. 'Our people will get the Government they voted for,' James Dillon had lamented. 'If it is Animal Farm they want they should vote for Fianna Fáil but if it is democracy and decency they want I suggest they will have to look elsewhere. I think the acceptance of corruption as the norm in public life is shocking.' Dillon was also quick to spot the threat to Lynch, whom he described as a young man of integrity, from some of his own cabinet Ministers. 'There is not an hour, or a day, or a week until they break his (Lynch's) heart, that the clash of knives will not be heard in the corridors of Fianna Fáil.'

It was not only Opposition TDs who were concerned about the trend in public life. In May 1967, George Colley, speaking at an Ógra Fianna Fáil conference in Galway urged those in attendance not to be dispirited 'if some people in high places appear to have low standards.' This was widely regarded as a reference to Haughey.

In opposition to this Labour had adopted the fashionable brand of 1960s socialism and attracted a number of high-profile figures like Conor Cruise O'Brien, David Thornley and Justin Keating into its ranks. Fine Gael too had also moved with the times and they adopted the 'Just Society' programme, espoused by reformers like Garret FitzGerald and Declan Costello. Fatally, though, Labour was still in an anti-coalition frame of mind and the voters did not have an alternative government on offer.

When Lynch called an election for June 1969, the country was offered a choice between the heady new policies of Fine Gael and Labour or a safe pair of hands to continue the policies that had brought relative prosperity to Ireland for the first time in the 1960s. Jack Lynch came into his own during the election campaign. His calmness, composure and basic decency might not have been respected by some of his more aggressive cabinet colleagues but they appealed to the electorate. When the votes were counted he was back in office with a bigger majority than that achieved by Lemass. Although Fianna Fáil's percentage share of the vote slipped, the party won 2 extra seats and had 75 in the 144 member Dáil. Fine Gael and Labour again increased their share of the vote. Combined they had almost 6% more than Fianna Fáil but, with Labour ruling out coalition, the election was again handed to Fianna Fáil.

The election victory boosted Lynch's authority but he was quickly plunged into a crisis that threatened not only his leadership but the stability of Irish democracy. The crisis arose directly from the eruption of widespread violence in the North. The IRA border campaign had ended with a whimper in 1961 due to lack of public support but discrimination against

Catholics in the North continued. In the late 1960s a group of Catholics decided to follow the example of the black civil rights movement in the US and they started a campaign for equal rights. Capt. O'Neill's gradual reform of the system had not removed the underlying sense of grievance and younger Catholics were impatient for change. A civil rights march in Derry in October 1968 was broken up by police and the same pattern was repeated through 1969. A counter reaction from loyalists provoked widespread rioting in Derry in August 1969. That was followed by a concerted Loyalist attack on Catholic areas of Belfast that forced thousands of people to flee their homes. Many of them fled across the border.

In response to the crisis Lynch promised that the Irish Government would not stand by and he set up a cabinet sub committee to coordinate policy on the North. What happened next is still in dispute but the outlines are clear. The cabinet sub committee was composed of Haughey, Blaney, Joe Brennan (from Donegal) and a young Minister from Louth, Padraig Faulkner. The sub committee met only once but it was used as a cover by Blaney and Haughey to embark on their own secret Northern policy. Blaney was the driving force and he opened links to the near moribund IRA through a young Army intelligence officer, Capt. James Kelly, who reported directly to him. Haughey as Minister for Finance had control of a £100,000 relief fund for the North. Delegations representing the besieged Catholics of Belfast pleaded with the two Ministers to supply arms for the defence of their communities. There was considerable sympathy in the Republic for the plight of Northern Catholics and Blaney and Haughey embarked on a plan to arm elements of the IRA as long as the organisation ceased activity in the Republic and focused on the North.

Some arms were supplied to the IRA but it was not until April 1970 that the issue came to a head when the civil servant in charge of the Department of Justice, Peter Berry, was informed about a plan to bring a large shipment of arms into the country through Dublin airport. He contacted Haughey and told him the arms would be seized if they arrived in Dublin. The plan was put on hold but Berry went to Lynch and told him of the conspiracy. Lynch, then and later, professed ignorance of the plan, even though it was known to senior members of the gardaí and the army and was widely spoken about in the republican movement. After receiving the information from Berry, Lynch went to Haughey and Blaney and asked them to resign but both men refused. The Taoiseach appeared to be paralysed by the gravity of the situation and took no further action until the Fine Gael leader, Liam Cosgrave, approached him with details of the conspiracy on 5 May 1970. That galvanised Lynch into action and he sacked Haughey and Blaney in the middle of the night. The public was stunned to wake up on 6 May to hear the news that the two most powerful Ministers in the cabinet had been fired.

Lynch may have responded belatedly to the crisis but once he decided to act he outwitted his opponents in Fianna Fáil at every turn. There was considerable sympathy in the party for the actions of Haughey and Blaney but Lynch isolated them by immediately demanding loyalty to himself as leader. The iron discipline of Fianna Fáil meant that even the two sacked Ministers voted confidence in Lynch and the Ministers he appointed to replace them. Haughey and Blaney were subsequently charged with conspiracy to import arms. Both men pleaded not guilty and proclaimed their ignorance of any plot. In separate trials they were found not guilty and for a brief period Lynch again appeared under threat but he managed to ride out the political storm. In November 1971 Blaney could not contain his disdain for Lynch and was eventually expelled from Fianna Fáil for failing to back the party in a Dáil vote. By contrast, Haughey swallowed his pride and hung on in the hope of better days to come, when he could realise his destiny by becoming leader of Fianna Fáil and eventually Taoiseach.

Lynch now in firm control of the party appointed George Colley as his Minister for Finance and put other loyal supporters in key positions. He picked a 30-year-old Limerick lawyer, Des O'Malley, for the key post of Minister for Justice. The brightest of the rising generation of Fianna Fáil politicians, O'Malley had the courage to take on the IRA and not to equivocate as some in Fianna Fáil would have preferred.

Violence spiralled out of control in the North after the 1969 riots and the British Government seemed helpless to deal with the issue even though the administration at Stormont proved ineffective. British troops were sent on to the streets to keep the peace, but they got sucked into the conflict and soldiers began to die. After the pogroms of 1969 the Provisional IRA gathered strength and launched a sustained terror campaign that in turn prompted loyalist death squads into action.

The one-sided introduction of internment without trial by Brian Faulkner's Stormont administration in 1971 prompted an escalation of violence from republicans. There was another flood of Catholic refugees to the Republic.

In January 1972, 13 men were shot dead during a civil rights march in Derry and the day became known as Bloody Sunday. The reaction throughout nationalist Ireland was intense. Crowds marched on the British Embassy in Dublin and after three days of protest the embassy was burned to the ground. As violence continued, two months later the British Government dissolved the Stormont administration and introduced direct rule. The Irish Government became deeply preoccupied with the problems in the North, particularly as loyalist bombs began to go off in Dublin.

Meanwhile negotiations to join the EEC proceeded to a successful conclusion. A referendum was held in the Republic in May 1972, and 83% of voters said 'Yes' to membership. Fianna Fáil and Fine Gael both supported a Yes vote although Labour campaigned against entry. The Party claimed that the EEC was a rich man's club, that jobs in protected industries would be lost and Irish sovereignty undermined. Some people in the Labour Party, notably Barry Desmond, Michael O'Leary and Conor Cruise O'Brien, were deeply unhappy at the stance and did not get involved in the campaign which was led by Justin Keating, Brendan Halligan and Michael Mullen of the ITGWU. Patrick Hillery, the Minister for Foreign Affairs, was outstanding in the Fianna Fáil campaign while Garret FitzGerald of Fine Gael dominated the public debates.

The gossip at the highest level in Fianna Fáil was that the President, Eamon de Valera, voted No, on the basis that he could not accept the diminution of the national sovereignty he had spent his life working for. It seems that he appreciated, as many others may have failed to do at the time, that joining the EEC was actually as momentous an event in Irish history as the signing of the Anglo-Irish Treaty in 1922. Ireland, Britain and Denmark joined the original six members of the EEC on 1 January 1973, completing the work sent in by Lemass. It started a process of transformation that would have exceeded Lemass's wildest dreams.

SEAN MACENTEE (1889–1984)

Sean MacEntee was one of the towering figures in Fianna Fáil. He was Minister for Finance in the first de Valera government in 1932, and was reappointed to that position 11 times. Famed as the most-long serving Minister, in what is regarded as the second most important position in government. MacEntee later became Tánaiste while Seán Lemass was Taoiseach.

MacEntee was born in Belfast and qualified as an engineer. He was also a poet of some promise. He took part in the 1916 Rising and was elected for the Monaghan constituency in the 1918 general election. He strongly opposed the Treaty on the basis that it would institutionalise partition and amount to the abandonment of Northern nationalists. He was one of the few TDs in the Treaty debate who referred to the issue at all. He was imprisoned during the Civil War but due to his close personal relations with the Free State Minister for Foreign Affairs, Desmond FitzGerald, he was given parole and allowed to go to France. A founder member of Fianna Fáil he represented various Dublin constituencies between 1927 and 1969.

A strictly orthodox Minister for Finance, he followed a tight budgetary policy that did nothing to alleviate the economic gloom of the 1950s. McEntee was a vituperative debater and was detested by the left for his red scare tactics in the 1940s and 1950s. He had a strained relationship with

Seán Lemass at times and was furious with him for the manner and timing of his departure from the party leadership. MacEntee was deeply suspicious of Charles Haughey from the beginning and did everything he could to support Jack Lynch during the arms crisis. A poet in his younger life, he was the father of the Irish language writer and poet, Maíre MacEntee, who later became the second wife of Conor Cruise O'Brien.

BOB BRISCOE (1894–1969)

A prominent Fianna Fáil TD for more than 30 years and a Lord Mayor of Dublin who attracted world-wide attention, Bob Briscoe was born in Dublin to Jewish parents of Lithuanian origin and was brought up in a strictly orthodox tradition. He was sent to the United States by his father in 1914 for fear of conscription but he returned home after the Rising in 1916 and he joined Fianna Éireann. He was active in the War of Independence and was sent by Michael Collins to buy guns in Germany and the US. He took the anti-Treaty side in the Civil War. A founder member of Fianna Fáil, Briscoe was elected as a TD for Dublin City South in 1927 and was returned at every election until 1965. His son, Ben, ran in that year and held the seat until 2002.

Bob Briscoe was prominent internationally as a supporter of Jewish causes, particularly the state of Israel. In 1939 he led a delegation of the World Zionist Organisation to seek international support for the settlement of Jews in Palestine. During his frequent trips to the US he became a well-known personality. There was particular interest in the fact that a Jew could become Lord Mayor of Dublin in 1956 in what was regarded as one of the most Catholic countries in the world. A television film about his life 'The Fabulous Irishman' was widely shown around the world.

His son Ben replaced him as a Fianna Fáil TD in 1965 and

played a prominent role in the party in the following decades. Most notably he proposed the motion of no confidence in Charles Haughey at a Fianna Fáil parliamentary meeting in January 1983. Like his father, he served as Lord Mayor of Dublin in 1988/89. In 1992 he held his seat by just five votes after a series of recounts lasting a week, thus ensuring that Fianna Fáil was returned to office. He did not contest the 2002 election.

CHAPTER EIGHT

THE COALITION ERA

Jack Lynch went to the country in February 1973, in the belief that the opposition parties were in no condition to fight an election. Fine Gael had been plunged into disarray in December 1972, when the party leader, Liam Cosgrave, decided to support tough anti-terrorist measures introduced by Lynch. The majority of Fine Gael TDs wanted to oppose the legislation and were on the point of ditching Cosgrave when loyalist bombs went off in Dublin. The party's TDs did a U turn and followed their leader, but it looked as if Cosgrave's days were numbered. Labour TDs had voted against the Bill and it seemed there was little likelihood the two opposition parties could come together to fight the election as an alternative Government.

Labour, though, had already made the decisive move to ditch its anti-coalition policy of the 1960s. The arms crisis convinced Corish and most leading members of his party that they had to offer the voters the prospect of an alternative government for conditions demanded it. Corish was hamstrung by a commitment that he would go to the backbenches rather than lead his party into coalition – but he found a way of getting off the hook. A special delegate conference of the Labour Party was convened in Cork in December 1970, to decide party policy on the issue of coalition. Dubbed 'Operation Houdini' by Conor Cruise O'Brien, the conference sanctioned a retreat from the principle of no coalition. Still, it took time for the two main opposition parties to come together. They campaigned on opposite sides in the 1972 Referendum on joining the EEC, with Fine Gael backing the Government proposal and Labour opposing it. With their differences on law and order coming on top of that, Lynch calculated that they would be in no position to come together to oppose him.

However, when the Taoiseach announced on 5 February 1973, that he had asked President de Valera to dissolve the Dáil, opposition minds were concentrated. Cosgrave and Corish knew it was their last chance of achieving office so they met and within minutes agreed to offer the electorate an alternative government. A 14-point plan, promising greater social justice but sticking to the Cosgrave line on law and order, was drafted without a hitch and the real campaigning began.

The biggest weapon Fine Gael and Labour had was that Fianna Fáil had been in office continuously for 16 years. As in 1948, enough voters simply wanted change and were prepared to take the risk of voting for a new and talented, if largely untested, team. The election took place on 28 February and when the votes were counted Fine Gael had gained 4 seats to 54 seats and Labour gained 1 to 19, giving the coalition a slim majority in the 144 member Dáil. Fianna Fáil dropped from 75 seats to 69, even though the party's share of the first preference vote actually went up while the combined Fine Gael and Labour vote went down. The critical thing was that the coalition deal generated good transfers between the two opposition parties.

Cosgrave was a very different Taoiseach to Jack Lynch. He was taciturn and uncompromising on what he regarded as the fundamental political issue, the security of the state. On most social and economic issues he was quite prepared to compromise with Labour but, as a deeply devout Catholic, he was not in tune with the liberal agenda that attracted leading Ministers of both coalition parties. Cosgrave was always his own man, regardless of political considerations or fashion. Most members of his cabinet were brilliant individuals and it quickly became known as 'the Government of all the talents.' Intellectuals like Garret FitzGerald at Foreign Affairs and Conor Cruise O'Brien at Posts and Telegraphs joined tough politicians like Richie Ryan at Finance and Jimmy Tully at Local Government to form a cohesive and reforming Government. As during the term of first inter-party Government, improvements were made in the welfare system, the health service was reorganised and a massive expansion in local authority house building was undertaken. In an attempt to distribute the wealth of society more evenly a controversial wealth tax, which upset wealthy Fine Gael supporters was introduced, and the PAYE tax system modernised.

The relationship between Cosgrave and Corish was the key to the successful operation of his Government. Despite their differences during the 1960s they trusted each other completely. 'They were practical people who weren't great intellectuals, who didn't have an awful lot to say and what they had to say they said to each other. Although it was a cabinet of all the talents those two guys were the ones in charge,' said the Government press secretary, Muris Mac Conghail.

An incident that illustrated their relationship happened one day in Leinster House when a scare developed about a possible coalition break-up. After a tetchy Cabinet meeting the rumour swept through the corridors that Cosgrave and Corish had adjourned for a crisis session. They were closeted together for so long in the Taoiseach's office that even some Ministers began to fear the worst. 'All the political correspondents had convinced themselves there was a Government crisis,' recalled Brendan Halligan, Labour's general secretary:

> Everybody was sure the game was up. The story suddenly swept the place. They had gone off together, nobody could get to them, it must be very serious and then of course you must find a justification for it. I walked into Leinster House in the middle of all this and I had guys jumping on me the minute I walked in the door. I went up and hammered away at the door of the Taoiseach's office and when I eventually got in I found the two boys were sitting there with a bottle of whiskey and looking at the horse racing from Cheltenham on the television. I eventually told them what everybody was saying and they were both just in fits of laughter. Now that sort of easy camaraderie was very important.

Racing was Cosgrave's passion, as it had been for his father before him. Ministers recall that the racing page of the *Irish Independent* was the only element of the media that he really cared about.

> He had a way of folding up the racing page and marking it that was quite distinctive. He marked his cabinet papers in the same way and it was not unusual for him to come to a cabinet meeting with the racing page wedged in between the other documents. There were even occasions, when the discussion was getting tedious, with Garret going on a bit, when he would slip out the racing page and study the form, said a former colleague.

Ireland had joined the EEC on 1 January 1973, and the Cosgrave Government had to take over the reins very quickly.

The country took to membership like a duck to water and much of the credit for that deservedly went to Garret FitzGerald, who showed that Ireland could make a positive and mature contribution to Europe. Although FitzGerald and Cosgrave had had a fraught relationship during the 1960s they worked well together in Government.

After a little over a year in office the coalition scored a spectacular own goal when it attempted to legalise contraception. A ban on the sale and importation of contraceptives had been introduced by de Valera in 1935 but by the late 1960s it had grown increasingly ridiculous in the eyes of many people and the law was widely flouted. In 1973 the Supreme Court decided the ban on importation was unconstitutional and the Minister for Justice, Patrick Cooney, responded by drafting a modest reform providing access to contraception for married people only. The Bill was opposed fiercely by Fianna Fáil whose TDs denounced the measure as the opening of the floodgates to the permissive society. The party imposed a three-line whip to ensure that all Fianna Fáil TDs would vote against it. The Government parties, on the suggestion of Labour, opted to have a free vote on what many regarded as a matter of conscience. It was widely expected that some conservative Fine Gael TDs like Oliver Flanagan, would oppose the Bill, but what astonished everyone was that the Taoiseach himself, without telling anybody in advance, also voted against his own Government's legislation. The Bill was defeated by 75 votes to 61.

Cosgrave was joined in the 'No' lobby by the Minister for Education, Dick Burke, and five other Fine Gael TDs. One Labour TD, Dan Spring, father of Dick, who was known to be opposed to the legislation did not travel to Dublin for the vote. Cosgrave had kept his opposition to the measure completely to himself and planned to vote last so that no one else would be swayed by his decision. That strategy came unstuck, however, because the Government chief whip, John Kelly only discovered after the vote had been called that his Taoiseach was going to vote against the Bill.

Garret FitzGerald recalls the general mood in the Cabinet: We had managed to convince ourselves that he would support the Bill when the time came … the chief whip, the late John Kelly, clearly had no qualms on the matter and was busy persuading the small number of anti-contraception Government TDs that they should vote for it, as, according to him, Liam Cosgrave was doing. What we did not realise was that John Kelly had no direct assurance from Liam Cosgrave but was, it seems, relying on an impression of his attitude gleaned from his private office, where the Taoiseach's position had apparently been misunderstood.

TDs had already begun passing through the lobbies when John discovered his error. Appalled at having misled some conservatively minded deputies into voting for the Bill on a false premise, he immediately urged the Taoiseach to vote without delay for, unaware of John Kelly's activities, Liam Cosgrave had loyally intended to wait until the end before casting his vote so as not to influence other members of the party. Once urged by John, he voted immediately against the Bill, and some who had not yet passed through the lobbies decided to follow him. By then, having voted, I was back on the front bench and, seeing what was happening, I said to

Pat Cooney. 'Wouldn't it be funny if he defeated the Government.' Not realising yet that this was what in fact had happened, recalled FitzGerald.

Another senior Minister, Peter Barry, also had no inkling of Cosgrave's intentions. 'He insisted this was a free vote but I thought he was protecting some of the backbenchers who had a problem. Blow me pink when I saw him walking up the stairs. You could have knocked me down. First of all I went pale but then you couldn't help feeling "well, fair dues." He believes in something, he knows the price he may have to pay for doing it.'

The Assistant Government Whip, Barry Desmond, a constituency colleague of the Taoiseach, had the dubious honour of recording the *Níl* vote in the Opposition lobby. He recalled his fellow Corkman, Jack Lynch remarking, as he passed through the lobby, 'A big own goal, Barry boy.'

Conor Cruise O'Brien recalled an amusing sequel:

The day after the vote two of my colleagues were discussing it in the early morning in Leinster House. They were talking about this with dismay, and how extraordinary and inexplicable it was, and one of the elderly cleaners listened to this stuff and just couldn't stick it and she veered back on her hunkers and she said: 'What are ye all talking about; surprised at the way he voted! Sure that man was an altar boy till he was 24.' And that was the whole story, he thought it was contrary to faith and morals.

It was one of the most remarkable episodes in the history of the Dáil and it left many of Cosgrave's Government colleagues dazed for a long time afterwards. The coalition's credibility took a severe knock and, while the Government continued in office for another three years, it never recovered its early confidence after the contraception debacle.

Northern Ireland was another big issue to face the Cosgrave Government in its early days. The Irish and British Government began intensive talks about how to establish a devolved power-sharing Government to the North, after the suspension of Stormont the year before. *Plus ça change.* The two Governments and the leaders of the Northern constitution met at Sunningdale in England in December 1973 to discuss a comprehensive settlement. A Unionist alliance led by Faulkner and the nationalist Social Democratic and Labour Party (SDLP) led by Gerry Fitt took part. Sinn Féin and the more militant loyalist groups were not invited because of their involvement in violence. Agreement was hammered out, involving the creation of a power-sharing executive in the North representing both communities. Faulkner was installed as Premier with Fitt as his deputy. There was also provision for cross-border cooperation on economic and security matters to be coordinated by a Council of Ireland representing North and South. It was a brave experiment but it lasted barely six months. The IRA continued its murderous campaign, fuelling discontent in the ranks of unionism. A strike organised by the Ulster Workers' Council of May 1974, undermined the Executive and the Labour Prime Minister, Harold Wilson, who had just been returned to office, lost his nerve and abandoned the experiment. Direct rule was restored.

In the Republic, the oil crisis, which followed the Arab-Israel war of October 1973, fuelled inflation and put the Government's economic policy off course. Through a combination of borrowing and tax increases, the economic situation was eventually stabilised but the Government became increasingly unpopular because of rising prices and unemployment. Minister for Finance Richie Ryan was dubbed 'Richie Ruin, the Minister for Hardship,' as prices spiralled out of control.

As the violence in the North escalated the security situation in the Republic remained a continuous worry. IRA activity in the shape of bank robberies, kidnappings and hunger strikes became the order of the day. One of the low points in the IRA terror campaign was the murder of the British Ambassador, Christopher Ewert-Biggs, who was killed in a bomb attack just outside his official residence at Glencairn in south county Dublin in July 1976. The incident was reminiscent of the Phoenix Park murders almost a century before. As in the 1880s the common reaction was one of horror but as time passed, the political atmosphere changed. Tough emergency legislation to deal with the IRA took time to draft and by the time it was debated in the Dáil Fianna Fáil and much of the media questioned its appropriateness.

The President, Cearbhall Ó Dálaigh, with whom Cosgrave had a poor relationship, referred the Bill to the Supreme Court, against the majority advice of his Council of State. There was fury among Government Ministers, although the Supreme Court – to the President's intense anger – found that the Bill was constitutional. The Minister for Defence, Paddy Donegan, described the President as 'a thundering disgrace' at an Army function in Mullingar. When the media reported the comment the President resigned and the credibility of the Government suffered.

Ó Dálaigh had only been in the President's office for two years. A former Attorney General and Chief Justice he was the agreed candidate for the Presidency when his predecessor Erskine Childers, died suddenly in 1974, having been elected the previous year. As the Fianna Fáil candidate for the job Childers had shown the fragility of Cosgrave's Government's position by easily winning the election against Tom O'Higgins in June 1973. After his sudden death, from a heart attack, the following year there was no stomach for another election and Cosgrave reluctantly accepted the nomination of Ó Dálaigh. Following Ó Dálaigh's resignation the major parties again side stepped an election by agreeing to appoint Ireland's first European Commissioner and former Minister for Foreign Affairs, Paddy Hillery, to the post. A reluctant President he ended up serving 14 years in the office because it suited both Fianna Fáil and Fine Gael.

A little over six months after the Ó Dálaigh fiasco, Cosgrave called a general election. He opted for June 1977, although some of his Ministers would have preferred to wait until the autumn. However, Corish wanted the June date and Cosgrave agreed to abide by his Tánaiste's wishes.

Fianna Fáil was well prepared and immediately published an election manifesto that contained the biggest give-away in Irish political history. It promised to abolish rates on houses and to end car tax. Hefty grants were promised for first-time house buyers and a huge expansion of the public service to create more jobs was also part of the plan. The abolition of the wealth tax, which had generated intense opposition from the country's wealthy elite, was also part of the package. With the country just coming out of the economic down turn caused by the oil crisis, the Fianna Fáil manifesto proved irresistible to the voters and the party won 50.6% of the vote, the second highest in its history. Jack Lynch, who had again proved a consummate election campaigner, came back with a whopping majority, winning 84 seats in the 144-member Dáil. Fine Gael dropped 9 seats to 43 while Labour lost 2 to end up with 17.

The election result was widely regarded as a big surprise because it was the last conducted in the absence of published opinion polls. Conventional political wisdom forecast a coalition victory on the basis of successful by-election results and the redrawing of the constituencies by Jimmy Tully, in a manner calculated to maximise Fine Gael and Labour seats. An attempt to manipulate the constituencies, dubbed the 'Tullymander' damaged the coalition's credibility and backfired in spectacular style to give Fianna Fáil a massive seat bonus. The scale of the victory actually stunned Lynch who immediately saw the potential for political instability from such a huge majority.

One significant promise made by Lynch during the election campaign in response to the 'Tullymander' was to establish an independent constituency commission to take the drawing of the boundaries out of the hands of the incumbent government for the first time. The implementation of that promise was to have far reaching consequences for Irish politics for the next 30 years because it made it extremely difficult for Fianna Fáil to win an overall majority.

While in opposition Lynch had bowed to internal party pressure in 1975 and brought Charles Haughey back on to the front bench. Forming his Government in the summer of 1977 Lynch felt he had no choice but to bring his enemy back into the cabinet and he made Haughey his Minister for Health. It was a fateful move because Haughey saw it as his long-awaited opportunity to make a determined push for the leadership. Haughey was helped by the fact that the implementation of the 1977 manifesto soon put the economic recovery under strain and Government borrowing started to climb. George Colley, the serious-minded Minister for Finance, honoured the give away elements of the manifesto which delivered higher public spending and tax concessions in an expectation of pay restraint that never materialised. In 1979, a second oil crisis, that led to a global economic slow down, compounded the Government's economic difficulties.

The long-term impact on the country of the rising tide of borrowing was to have devastating consequences for more than a decade.

Following the defeat of the coalition, Cosgrave resigned and was replaced as leader of Fine Gael by the dynamic Garret FitzGerald. An economics lecturer at UCD, FitzGerald had been a hugely successful Minister for Foreign Affairs. Committed to Fine Gael's Just Society programme of the 1960s he was a breath of fresh air and he quickly managed to revitalise his party, even though he came from its liberal fringe rather than its centre. Corish resigned as Labour leader and was replaced by Frank Cluskey, a tough, witty, Dublin trade unionist. He didn't have FitzGerald's dash but he was a fine Dáil performer. His major problem was that the Labour Party was full of talented but prickly individuals who found it difficult to work as a team.

Haughey started campaigning for the leadership of Fianna Fáil from the moment he came back to the cabinet. Many of the newly elected TDs could see that the economic policy was not working and, after a poor showing in the first direct elections to the European Parliament in the summer of 1979, they concluded that a change of leader was essential. Síle de Valera, the granddaughter of the chief, a TD and a member of the European Parliament, made a bellicose speech attacking Lynch's policy on the North. New TDs like Albert Reynolds, Padraig Flynn and Sean Doherty who had made the breakthrough into national politics in 1977 supported Haughey as did younger men like Bertie Ahern and Charlie McCreevy. The new TDs saw in Haughey's accession a fast track to the top for themselves.

Lynch had intended to step down in early 1980 and was hoping to pass the baton to Colley. However, Colley sensed that Haughey was gaining momentum with each passing month and he persuaded Lynch to resign a bit earlier to try and wrong foot the Haughey camp. The tactic backfired.

When the secret ballot was taken, on 7 December 1979, Haughey won by 44 votes to 38. It was closer than Haughey had expected but there was no taking from his triumph and from the shock and bewilderment of the party hierarchy who were convinced up to the end that Colley would win. The shattered Colley and his supporters didn't know what to do. Such was the depth of distrust of Haughey that over the next few days Colley had long discussions with leading colleagues like Martin O'Donoghue and Des O'Malley to consider whether he would even vote for his rival's nomination for Taoiseach. When it came to the vote on 11 December he did vote for Haughey but the palpable hostility of the different factions in Fianna Fáil prompted an extraordinary speech from

Fine Gael leader, Garret FitzGerald.

> I must speak not only for the opposition but for many in Fianna Fáil who may not be free to say what they believe or to express their deep fears for the future of this country under the proposed leadership, people who are not free to reveal what they know and what led them to oppose this man with a commitment far beyond the normal.

FitzGerald went on to refer to Haughey's 'flawed pedigree' and said his motives could ultimately only be judged by God.

> But we cannot ignore the fact that he differs from all his predecessors in that those motives have been and are widely impugned, most notably but by no means exclusively, by people within his own party, people close to him who have observed his actions for many years and who have made their human interim judgement on him … The feet that will go through that lobby to support his election will include many that will drag; the hearts of many who will climb those stairs before turning left will be heavy. Many of those who may vote for him will be doing so in the belief and hope that they will not have to serve long under a man they do not respect, whom they have fought long and hard, but for the moment in vain, to exclude from the highest office in the land.

Ironically, the speech did more damage to him than to Haughey but time would prove FitzGerald right. In December 1979 FitzGerald not only got to the heart of the matter, he very accurately reflected the mood in the defeated faction within Fianna Fáil.

PEOPLE, POLITICS AND POWER

DECLAN COSTELLO (1926-)

A politician and lawyer, Costello was the inspiration behind the 'Just Society' document that had a profound influence on Fine Gael for decades after its publication. Described as 'intense, intellectual, shy and unclubbable' by party colleague and historian, Maurice Manning, he served as a TD and as Attorney General in the Cosgrave Government of the 1970s before becoming a High Court and then a Supreme Court judge. His lasting influence on politics was through his pioneering work in developing policy rather than through direct political action.

The son of John A. Costello, who was twice Taoiseach, Declan was first elected to the Dáil for Dublin North West in 1951. He represented the constituency until 1969 when he retired temporarily from politics before returning in 1973 as a TD for Dublin South West. After Fine Gael's defeat in the 1957 election Costello established a Research and Information Centre within the party that published a newspaper called the *National Observer*. At a time when Ireland was still largely isolated from developments in the world outside, the Centre became the forum for debating new ideas about politics and state planning.

Costello believed that Fine Gael would go nowhere unless it came up with a clear set of alternative policies to those being implemented by Fianna Fáil. He made a determined effort to shift his party to the left and the result was the 'Just Society' programme of 1964, which committed Fine Gael to a range of actions in support of social justice. Although it met with considerable internal resistance the document helped to pave the way for the coalition with Labour in 1973 and for the policies adopted by Costello's political ally, Garret FitzGerald, when he became Taoiseach in the 1980s. As Attorney General in the Cosgrave Government, Costello implemented a fundamental reform in the administration of justice in Ireland through the creation of the non-political office of the Director of Public Prosecutions.

CONOR CRUISE O'BRIEN (1917-)

Politician, civil servant, academic, writer and journalist, Conor Cruise O'Brien left an indelible impression on Irish public life – although he was very much on the minority side in most of the controversies in which he participated. His greatest achievement was to lead the way in challenging traditional nationalist assumptions about partition and providing a fierce critique of republican violence. The controversial and unconventional opinions about Irish nationalism that he propounded in the early 1970s became the conventional wisdom of the 1990s, although by then he had embarked on an ill-advised flirtation with extreme Unionism.

Born in Dublin in 1917, his mother, Kathleen, was the daughter of the politician David Sheehy. Through her he was related to the Sheehy-Skeffingtons and Tom Kettle. He emerged from Trinity College as one of the most brilliant intellectuals of his generation and joined the Department of Foreign Affairs. Ironically, in view of his later career, his formidable talents were deployed in the anti-partition campaign waged by successive governments in the late 1940s and early 1950s.

He made an impression as an Irish diplomat at the United Nations after Ireland joined in 1956. He came to world prominence as a special representative of the UN secretary general, Dag Hammarskjold, when Katanga tried to secede from what is now the Democratic Republic of Congo. When the Congo crisis spun out of control he resigned and wrote *To Katanga and Back* (1962), which has become a classic of modern African history.

After stints as Chancellor of the University of Ghana and New York University he returned to Ireland and was elected to the Dáil as a Labour Party TD in 1969 for the same constituency as Charles Haughey. He had a huge influence on Labour's Northern policy and on the formation of the Fine Gael-Labour coalition in 1973, and he was appointed Minister for Posts and Telegraphs. His unremitting critique of Irish republicanism generated a great deal of controversy, particularly the banning of Sinn Féin and IRA members from direct access to radio and television. He lost his seat in 1977 but was elected to the Seanad for one term. In 1979 he was appointed editor-in-chief of *The Observer* newspaper (UK). In the mid 1990s he was elected to the Northern Ireland Forum for the UK Unionist Party. He later resigned from the party after suggesting that Unionists should think about a united Ireland as a means of avoiding rule by Sinn Féin.

His most important books include *States of Ireland* (1972), *The Great Melody, a biography of Edmund Burke*, (1992) and a memoir *My Life and Themes* (1998).

RICHARD MULCAHY (1886–1971)

Richard (Dick) Mulcahy will always be remembered for two things: as Minister for Defence and Chief of Staff of the Army. After the death of Michael Collins in August 1922, Mulchay prosecuted the Civil War to a successful conclusion and ensured that the Free State was put on a firm foundation. Later in his career, when he was leader of Fine Gael, he stepped aside and allowed a colleague become Taoiseach in order to ensure that his party entered government in 1948. The two critical periods in his public life were linked, because it was his role in the Civil War that prevented him from becoming Taoiseach.

Mulcahy was born in Waterford and joined the Post Office as a young man. In Dublin he joined the Irish Volunteers and in 1916 was the second in command to Thomas Ashe in a bloody encounter with the RIC at Ashbourne. He became chief of staff of the Irish Volunteers in March 1918, and was elected as MP for Clontarf in the 1918 general election. A supporter of the Treaty, he was appointed Minister for Defence and also took over the Army after the death of Collins. In both positions he was strongly associated with the policy that resulted in the execution of 77 republicans.

He succeeded WT Cosgrave as leader of Fine Gael in 1944, at a time when the party was demoralised and in decline after a succession of election defeats. After the 1948 election he saw the possibilities of putting the Inter-Party Government together but realised that agreement would not be possible under his leadership, because of the hostility of Clann na Poblachta and Labour over his Civil War record. He helped persuade John A. Costello to take the Taoiseach's office and he became Minister for Education in both Inter-Party Governments. He resigned the party leadership in 1959.

Paradoxically, through marriage with Josephine Ryan he had strong family ties with his Civil War opponents. His wife's sister married Sean T. O'Kelly, Fianna Fáil Minister and later President of Ireland, while her brother was James Ryan, a leading Fianna Fáil Minister and confidant of de Valera.

CHAPTER NINE

DEADLY RIVALS

Politics for the next decade was dominated by the antagonism between Haughey and FitzGerald and the deep animosity of a minority in Fianna Fáil for their new leader. Haughey and FitzGerald were polar opposites in almost every way, political, social and personal but they brought an excitement and a passion to Irish politics that has not been seen since. Despite the fact that they were born within months of each other, were educated together in UCD and knew each other from that time they had virtually nothing in common. Haughey was a Dublin northsider, a Christian Brothers boy, a GAA supporter, who had become rich quickly by dubious means and believed in flaunting that wealth and aping the behaviour of the landed gentry.

By contrast FitzGerald was a product of the new Catholic elite that took over the running of the country after the British left. Both his parents took part in the 1916 Rising and his father, Desmond, was Minister for External Affairs from 1922 to 1927, representing Ireland at the League of Nations and Imperial conferences. FitzGerald was brought up in the comfortable middle-class surroundings of Dublin's south side and was educated by the Jesuits before going on to UCD, and never set foot in Croke Park until he became Taoiseach. He entered politics because he wanted to change Ireland in line with his vision of a modern, tolerant European democracy coming to an accommodation with the North rather than sticking to the old mantra about a united Ireland. Despite his political pedigree he was not really a party politician and had voted for Lemass in 1961. He only joined Fine Gael rather than Labour because he saw in the bigger party an opportunity to achieve what he wanted in politics.

The contrast between the leaders' backgrounds heightened their distrust of each other and contributed to a mutual lack of comprehension. The gulf also accentuated the intensity of Haughey's appeal to traditional working-class and rural voters who rallied to his nationalist rhetoric. FitzGerald, by contrast, broadened Fine Gael's appeal beyond its traditional base attracting middle-class liberal voters and women in significant numbers.

One of the reasons Haughey aroused such antagonism from FitzGerald and senior people in Fianna Fáil was that they genuinely feared that he would corrupt the standards of public life. His record in the arms trial added to those fears. The fact that Haughey possessed charisma, as well as great leadership ability made him all the more dangerous in the eyes of his opponents.

The source of Haughey's vast wealth was a mystery. He lived an extravagant lifestyle that was clearly way in excess of his income as a public representative yet there was no visible means of support for that lordly lifestyle. Shortly before he took over as party leader he bought Inishvickillane, one of the Blasket islands and was busy building a house on the beautiful site. There were all sorts of rumours about how Haughey had acquired wealth during the 1960s and, while the truth was only known to a handful of people, the popular perception was that he had obtained it by dubious means. Haughey's reputation seemed strangely to appeal to many and far from damaging his standing the whiff of sulphur surrounding his wealth and his record in the arms trial, proved a powerful attraction for many voters.

Haughey's first task was to select a new cabinet and he was initially conciliatory to the most powerful of his sworn enemies in the senior ranks of the party although he did drop some Ministers, including Martin O'Donoghue, who had been a protégé of Lynch. In an incident worthy of a gangster film O'Donoghue received a special delivery at his home a couple of days after he had been axed. Haughey's garda driver arrived at O'Donoghue's home in Rathgar and handed a strange parcel to his wife. When the couple opened it they found two dead ducks inside, along with a curt message from Haughey. 'Shot on my estate this morning'. O'Donoghue regarded the delivery as a menacing gesture and not simply a joke in bad taste.

Haughey's chief supporters, Ray MacSharry and Albert Reynolds, were rewarded with cabinet office in his first Government. Another new face in the cabinet was Máire Geoghegan-Quinn who was the only other junior Minister, apart from MacSharry to back Haughey. She was the first woman cabinet Minister since Countess Markievicz in 1918.

One of Haughey's first actions was to make a television address warning that the country's finances were spinning out of control. 'The figures which are just now becoming available to us show one thing very clearly. As a community we are living way beyond our means,' Haughey told the nation. 'We have been borrowing enormous amounts of money, borrowing at a rate which just cannot continue. We will just have to reorganise Government spending so that we can only undertake those things we can afford.' Given what emerged over a decade later about Haughey's personal finances at the time, the speech was a piece of brazen effrontery.

The diagnosis was correct but having identified the problem Haughey proceeded to do precisely the opposite. He failed to curb Government spending and borrowing and conceded large pay increases to the public service. Things got worse in 1981 and the budget figures were massaged to disguise the fact that borrowing was on course to the unsustainable level of 20% of GNP.

FitzGerald kept up a sustained criticism of Haughey's economic policies and there was also a huge gulf between them on the issue of Northern Ireland. Haughey had always regarded the national issue as the one which was the key to his place in the history books. He reportedly told the British Prime Minister, Margaret Thatcher, during their first meeting in 1980 that no political leader would be remembered for reducing the balance of payments or for adjusting the scale of Government borrowing, but the one who came up with a solution to the problem of the North would go down in the history. Given his role in the arms crisis of 1970 and his nationalist rhetoric Haughey, during his early years as leader, was regarded within Fianna Fáil as being 'sound' on the national question. Attending his first ard fheis as leader in February 1980 he was greeted to an ecstatic welcome from more than 5000 delegates. He was piped into the RDS by the ITGWU brass band to the strains of 'A Nation Once Again'. His speech, which reflected traditional Fianna Fáil attitudes to the North, was greeted with hysteria by the audience.

In the front row people even erected little shrines to Haughey, with photographs and posters on tables they had pillaged from the press area, and their devotion had a religious fervour. In his speech Haughey coined the phrase that Northern Ireland was 'a failed political entity' and he called on the British Government to declare its interest in encouraging the unity of Ireland. That first ard fheis set the tone of adulation for him among the party organisation that lasted most of his time as leader.

Haughey's emphasis on the traditional goal of a united Ireland contrasted sharply with FitzGerald's support for a devolved power sharing arrangement in Northern Ireland as the first step towards any solution. From the beginning of his first term as Taoiseach, Haughey maintained that decisions could only be taken by the two Governments over the heads of the squabbling parties in the North. Haughey astounded his critics, particularly FitzGerald, by making a good stab at fulfilling his dream of launching a major political initiative. After six months in office he met Margaret Thatcher, herself in her first year in Government, for an Anglo-Irish summit meeting in London. He brought her an antique Irish silver teapot as a present and despite the jokes and the ridicule that followed about 'teapot diplomacy' the leaders got off to a good start.

The really significant follow-up summit took place in December 1980 in Dublin Castle. The joint communiqué issued after the meeting described the talks as 'extremely constructive and significant' and went on to say that the 'totality of relationships' between the two islands would be considered in a number of joint studies. Haughey made it clear that he was even prepared to consider a defence pact with Britain in the context of agreement on the North. 'We would, of course, have to review what would be the most appropriate defence arrangements for these islands as a whole. It would be unrealistic and improvident not to,' he told the Dáil. The meeting with Thatcher heralded a genuinely important breakthrough. It paved the way for the Anglo-Irish agreement signed by FitzGerald in 1985 and for the peace process of the 1990s. Haughey could have brought much of this about himself in the period after the Dublin summit but he showed crass political judgement as he proceeded to dissipate the achievement by insisting that the constitutional position of Northern Ireland as part of the UK was now in the melting pot.

As on the economy Haughey squandered his opportunities in Anglo-Irish relations by taking a populist line directed towards winning an overall majority for himself in his first general election as Fianna Fáil leader. By early 1981 he had decided to call the election in the spring of that year, while he was still riding the crest of the popular wave, but his plans were thwarted by tragedy, not once but twice. The initial plan was to call the election shortly after the party's ard fheis in February but on the opening night of the conference, St Valentine's night, a fire in the Stardust nightclub in the Taoiseach's own constituency killed 48 young people. The main part of the ard fheis, including the Taoiseach's address was postponed until April as were his election plans.

Then the North intervened in an unexpected way to throw a spanner in the works. One of the British responses to continuing IRA violence was to withdraw 'special category' status from IRA prisoners convicted after March 1976. This provoked first, a dirty protest, and then a hunger strike that led to escalating tension. Hunger strike leader Bobby Sands was elected to the Commons in a by-election in Fermanagh-South Tyrone in April and died the following month. Haughey's Government made furious but unavailing efforts to try and end the hunger strikes and again deferred his election plans.

With his options closing down and the spending targets of the 1981 Budget running way out of control Haughey dissolved the Dáil on 21 May with the general election to be held on 11 June. It was to be the first of five elections during the 1980s. During the election campaign Fianna Fáil continued to promise the electorate more spending programmes to rival the attractive, if equally unrealistic, tax cutting plans being put forward by Fine Gael. Haughey and FitzGerald ran presidential style campaigns and dominated the media coverage. 'Charlie's Song', a version of a folk song about Bonny Prince Charlie, became the Fianna Fáil campaign anthem and it was played at all the party rallies during the campaign encouraging voters to 'Arise and follow Charlie'. Fianna Fáil spirits soared in the early days of the campaign when an IMS opinion poll put the party on 52% of the vote. Haughey looked all set for a smashing victory, but in a pattern which was to repeat itself support ebbed during the rest of the campaign.

Fine Gael's tax cutting promises and the swell of sympathy for H Block hunger strike candidates all played their part in cutting Haughey's early lead. The media began to give him a tough time during the campaign. Irritated by his arrogant style many of the reporters covering his tour of the country developed an antipathy to him.

It was a fiercely fought and close election. Fine Gael and Labour did not have a formal pact but it was widely expected that they would form a Government if they had the numbers. Haughey campaigned hard around the country with huge crowds attending his rallies. Fine Gael was rejuvenated just four years after the disaster of 1977 but Labour was marginalised by the intensity of the battle between FitzGerald and Haughey. An unknown factor in the equation was the emergence of hunger strikers as election candidates.

The result was close but Haughey was squeezed out of power. The Fianna Fáil vote was down 5% and the party won 78 seats in a 166 member Dáil. Fine Gael was up 5% and the party took 65 seats, Labour slipped to just under 10% but won 15 seats, although the party leader, Frank Cluskey, lost his seat. Hunger strike candidates won two seats and effectively deprived Haughey of any chance of power. Fine Gael and Labour were four seats short of a Dáil majority but Garret FitzGerald was elected Taoiseach with the support of three Independents.

FitzGerald and the new Labour leader, Michael O'Leary, quickly negotiated a programme for government – but it was only endorsed by Labour after a stormy delegate conference. O'Leary was a charming and charismatic Corkman who was elected as a TD for Dublin Central in 1965 and became a leading Labour figure in the years that followed. His support for Corish's U turn on coalition carried deep suspicions about him on the Labour left. Haughey's economic mismanagement presented the new Government with enormous problems but the Fianna Fáil leader refused to be embarrassed by his record. Instead he denounced the new Government's corrective measures as deflationary and monetarist, rejecting what he called their attitude of 'gloom and doom'. An air of political crisis hung over the first FitzGerald Government.

For a start the new Minister for Finance, John Bruton, was obliged by Haughey's profligacy to introduce an emergency budget in July 1981, to prevent the country careering into bankruptcy. That involved Fine Gael jettisoning most of its tax cutting election promises in the face of economic reality. As the hunger strikers began to die Sinn Féin organised street protests in Dublin and a serious attempt was made to attack the British Embassy in Ballsbridge. There were violent street scenes as the gardaí repelled rioters and ensured that the embassy was not burned down for the second time in a decade. So determined was the cabinet to prevent this happening that an Army detachment was secretly stationed behind the embassy walls with full authority to use necessary force if required.

Drafting the budget for January 1982 presented John Bruton with an array of problems, the main one being to get the public finances under control while fulfilling some of the pledges on social justice in his government's programme. In order to fund a 25% increase in social welfare payments demanded by Labour, Bruton opted to extend VAT to clothing and footwear and to abolish food subsidies. Both of these measures were regarded as sensible by almost all economists and were adopted by subsequent governments. However, in January 1982 they prompted a sensational defeat for the Government when two of the Independents on which it relied, Sean 'Dublin Bay' Loftus and Jim Kemmy voted against the budget. FitzGerald had no option but to dissolve the Dáil and call an election for February 1982.

On the night of the budget defeat, a series of events took place that were to have an enormous influence on politics almost a decade later. After the Government was defeated, the Fianna Fáil front bench met and a statement was issued calling on President Hillery not to grant a dissolution of the Dáil but to look to Fianna Fáil to form a Government. Phone calls were then made from the Fianna Fáil rooms in Leinster House to Áras an Uachtaráin to reinforce the message. The President ignored the calls and granted FitzGerald his dissolution – but the issue would come back to haunt Irish politics.

Haughey got back into power by the skin of his teeth in February 1982 but he still didn't have an overall majority. The Fianna Fáil vote went up to 47.3% and the party gained 3 seats to 81. After an intense campaign on the issue of fiscal rectitude, the Fine Gael vote went up, but the party lost 2 seats to end up on 63. Labour held its own with 15 seats while the number of Independents dropped from 7 to 4. Ironically, Sean 'Dublin Bay' Loftus, who had helped to bring the Government down, lost the seat he had held for just six months and was never to regain it.

Surprisingly, Haughey was put back into office by four left wing TDs. The first was the Independent Socialist, Tony Gregory, who got a deal for his impoverished Dublin Central constituency. The other three were members of Sinn Féin the Workers Party (SFWP) which had its roots in the 1970 split in the republican movement. The 1982 election marked the breakthrough for the SFWP, which was committed to a socialist analysis of the economy and total opposition to the IRA's campaign of violence.

Immediately after the election the first in a succession of heaves was launched against Haughey's leadership. It collapsed quickly but the divisions in Fianna Fáil were obvious for all to see. Haughey recast his cabinet, appointing the tough-minded Ray MacSharry to Finance. This was the first sign that he was finally taking the economic crisis seriously. While MacSharry initially proclaimed that he intended to replace 'gloom and doom' with 'boom and bloom' he quickly grasped the state of the public finances and started to devise a comprehensive plan to deal with the problem. This emerged in the autumn in the form of a document called 'The Way Forward' which spelled out a series of tough measures to get the economy back on track.

However, by that stage Haughey's Government was collapsing around his ears after a nine-month roller coaster characterised by internal dissent, political crises and bizarre happenings. Most of the strange events happened in the Department of Justice where Haughey appointed Sean Doherty, one of the class of '77, as a Minister after just five years in the Dáil. A charming, freewheeling former detective in awe of his boss and prepared to bend the rules, Doherty was considered a loose cannon in a very sensitive position.

A Garda sergeant in Doherty's constituency was threatened with a move to a remote area for trying to implement pub closing times. Mysterious things happened in a court case involving the Minister's brother-in-law. More seriously there were rumours about the phones of journalists and Haughey's opponents being tapped as part of the internal row in Fianna Fáil.

As if that was not enough the country's most wanted man, double murderer, Malcolm McArthur, was found by gardaí holed up in the apartment of none other than Haughey's Attorney General, Patrick Connolly. McArthur was arrested after a man hunt that had lasted for weeks and, given the level of paranoia in the country at the time, all sorts of speculation took hold. Haughey characterised the event as 'grotesque, unbelievable, bizarre and unprecedented' and from those words Conor Cruise O'Brien coined the acronym GUBU. The newly minted word perfectly described the sinister atmosphere of the summer and autumn of 1982. The Attorney General who had no knowledge of McArthur's crimes had to resign his position to save the government further embarrassment.

The GUBU chain of events encouraged Haughey's long standing internal critics to think once more of removing him as leader. Those who had opposed his leadership from the beginning were joined by other discontented TDs including Charlie McCreevy, who had helped plot Haughey's accession to power but had been openly critical of Haughey's economic policies. Late on the night of Friday, 1 October 1982, McCreevy put down a motion of no confidence in Haughey for the following Wednesday's weekly meeting of the parliamentary party.

All sides were caught on the hop. Leading anti-Haughey figures like Des O'Malley and George Colley were as taken aback as the Haughey loyalists like Ray MacSharry, Albert Reynolds and Bertie Ahern, who had risen quickly to the key post of chief whip. The Fianna Fáil organisation rallied to the support of the party leader and intense pressure was applied to any TD believed to be wavering against the leadership. Dissident TDs again received intimidating phone calls and threats from Haughey's supporters. There was no secret ballot but an open roll call vote that Haughey won by 58 votes to 22. When the result of the vote was announced in Leinster House the place went wild. Haughey supporters who had been piling into the House all evening were ecstatic and some of them were drunk. As the TDs came down into the main hall there was a tremendous crush as reporters and Fianna Fáil supporters struggled to get near the participants. When Haughey's most implacable opponent, Jim Gibbons, appeared and tried to make his way towards the door he was surrounded by a crowd of angry Haughey supporters. One of them struck Gibbons and a group of Dáil ushers had to swoop in to protect him and escort him to his car. The unruly crowd spilled out into the car park and other anti-Haughey TDs, quickly dubbed the 'Club of 22' got rough treatment. McCreevy was chased across the car park, kicked and jostled and called a 'bastard' and a 'blueshirt'. The gardaí helped him to get into his car but the crowd surrounded it banging on the roof and shouting insults as he drove away through the Kildare Street gates of Leinster House.

Haughey had seen off his internal critics for the second time in less than a year but his minority Government's position became precarious with the death of Clare TD, Bill Loughnane, two weeks later. It was followed by the hospitalisation of Gibbons who suffered a severe heart attack not long after the traumatic attack on him in Leinster House. When the Government committed itself to the substantial cuts in public spending in 'The Way Forward' Independent left wing TD, Tony Gregory, and the Workers Party withdrew their support. Fine Gael moved to capitalise on the Government's difficulty by tabling a motion of no confidence. When the vote was taken on 4 November the Government was defeated by 82 votes to 80 and an election was fixed for 24 November.

Just before the election was called the Labour Party suffered its own trauma. The party leader, Michael O'Leary, had grown increasingly weary of the incessant battles over coalition and he asked the party's annual conference in Galway at the end of October 1982 to give the elected TDs a free hand to decide the issue. The conference rejected his proposal and O'Leary promptly resigned as a Labour TD and joined Fine Gael. A stunned Labour parliamentary party then elected the 32-year-old TD for Kerry North, Dick Spring, who had been in the Dáil for just over a year, as its new leader. It was a baptism of fire for him.

The third election in 18 months finally produced a decisive result with Fine Gael and Labour winning a clear majority. Fine Gael won 39% of the vote and 70 seats in the party's best showing since its foundation in 1933. The Labour vote held steady and the party won an extra seat bringing its total to 16 and giving the coalition parties a clear majority. The Fianna Fáil votes slipped to 45% with the party winning 75 seats.

Almost immediately after the election Haughey faced yet another challenge to his leadership. After the change of Government the new Minister for Justice, Michael Noonan, launched an immediate investigation into the behaviour of his predecessor Sean Doherty. The findings were sensational. Noonan announced on 20 January 1983 that the phones of political journalists, Geraldine Kennedy and Bruce Arnold, had been tapped on the instructions of Doherty and that normal procedures had not been followed. Even more surprising – he also disclosed that Ray MacSharry had borrowed Garda equipment to secretly record a conversation with Martin O'Donoghue in October 1982. Fianna Fáil was immediately plunged into another crisis and this time few gave Haughey a chance of surviving. A special party meeting was held on Sunday, 23 January to discuss the implications of the revelations. When the Dáil resumed the following Wednesday there was widespread speculation that Haughey would resign.

The crucial party meeting took place on 7 February 1983. Crowds gathered on Kildare Street throughout the day as Fianna Fáil TDs debated the issue from 11.00 am until midnight. Much of the time at the meeting was spent by Haughey loyalists attacking the media and the leader's opponents. This time around there was a secret ballot but while the vote was closer it still gave the same result as the open vote in October. Haughey won by 40 votes to 33. Pandemonium ensued as Haughey emerged triumphant and made his way through Leinster House to the main gate to greet the crowd that had gathered to support him.

In the meantime the Fine Gael-Labour coalition tried to get to grips with the country's problems. The coalition had a mandate to act but was fatally paralysed on the central economic issue facing the country – the state of the public finances. Fine Gael had committed itself to public spending cuts as the only way out of the economic morass but the scale of the cutbacks required was vehemently opposed by Spring who publicly challenged the budgetary strategy of the new Minister for Finance, Alan Dukes. FitzGerald backed the Labour position and the result was a stalemate that paralysed Government economic policy for the next four years. Dukes did stop the national debt spiralling out of control, and actually began to get it down as a percentage of GNP. This was achieved by punishing levels of taxation, rather than by spending cuts, and the result was rapidly rising unemployment. There were unsettling echoes of the 1950s as serious emigration began again.

FitzGerald's second major objective was a 'constitutional crusade' to liberalise Irish society. He made a disastrous start to this because of a commitment he gave during the election to support the introduction of a constitutional ban on abortion. The wording of the amendment was drafted by the Haughey Government and while FitzGerald accepted it initially, he had second thoughts and decided to oppose it. His party split, as did Labour, and the Fianna Fáil amendment was carried. His Government had more success liberalising the law on contraception due to the tenaciousness of the Labour Minister for Health, Barry Desmond. He swept away a law introduced by Haughey in 1979, and famously described by him as 'an Irish solution to an Irish problem' that only allowed married people to legally buy contraceptives. On divorce FitzGerald led a referendum campaign in 1986 to try and have the ban lifted but the proposal was defeated after fierce opposition from Fianna Fáil.

It was only on his third major objective of making progress on Northern Ireland that FitzGerald had an unqualified success. The Anglo-Irish Agreement of 1985 provided for a direct input by the Irish Government into the running of the North. It provided an institutional framework for the Irish Government to put forward its views and proposals on how the North should be administered and it ultimately led to the IRA ceasefire nearly a decade later.

Haughey fought tooth and nail against everything FitzGerald attempted, on the economy, the liberal agenda and the North.

He denounced the Anglo-Irish Agreement as unconstitutional, claiming that it would copper fasten partition and that he would renegotiate it if returned to office. He repeatedly denounced FitzGerald as 'Thatcherite' and 'monetarist'. Haughey won the propaganda war by having it accepted that FitzGerald's Government doubled the national debt. In fact in real terms the coalition actually stopped it from rising. Politics was dominated by the economy and the state of the public finances during this period. In 1977 the national debt stood at €5.3 billion or 70% of GNP. By 1987 it had soared to €30 billion or 118% of GNP.

FitzGerald's problem was that the medicine used to tackle the debt crisis was disproportionately reliant on taxation, and the economic consequences in terms of rising unemployment and low growth were disastrous. The air of depression in the mid 1980s was heightened by the fact that the only alternative to an increasingly unpopular Fine Gael-Labour coalition seemed to be a Fianna Fáil Government committed to economic profligacy, conservative social policies and a reactionary Northern policy.

It was this nightmare scenario that prompted the foundation of a new party called the Progressive Democrats, led by Des O'Malley. O'Malley was expelled from Fianna Fáil for refusing to toe the party line and vote against Barry Desmond's Family Planning Bill that finally legalised contraception. In an electrifying speech to the Dáil, O'Malley showed his disgust at what he regarded as the opportunistic and reactionary policy being followed by Haughey:

The politics of this would be very easy. The politics would be, to be one of the lads, the safest way in Ireland. But I do not believe that the interests of this State, or our Constitution and of this Republic would be served by putting politics before conscience in regard to this. There is a choice of a kind that can only be answered by saying that I stand by the Republic and accordingly, I will not oppose this Bill.

O'Malley was expelled from Fianna Fáil in February 1985 for 'conduct unbecoming' and in December of that year he presided at the launch of the PDs. The key movers behind the new party were Mary Harney, a Fianna Fáil TD, who was expelled for supporting the FitzGerald line on the North, and Michael McDowell, a prominent Fine Gael activist who had become utterly disillusioned with FitzGerald's approach to the economic crisis. O'Malley, Harney and McDowell were to have a profound effect on the course of Irish politics for the next two decades but when they launched the PDs just before Christmas 1985, few gave them much chance of surviving their first election.

CHAPTER TEN

BIRTH OF THE CELTIC TIGER

Charles Haughey got his third chance at power in 1987 and finally showed what he was capable of. The election of February 1987 was initially a huge disappointment to Fianna Fáil. Despite a long campaign denouncing the FitzGerald Government's policies and a dramatic billboard campaign proclaiming: 'Cuts hurt the old, the poor and the handicapped' Haughey again failed to win an overall majority. Fianna Fáil won 81 seats, an increase of 6, but it was well short of the sweeping majority the opinion polls had predicted. Fine Gael fell back to 51 seats, a drop of 19, and Labour won just 12, down 4. Party leader Dick Spring almost lost his seat in Kerry North and only survived by four votes. The big story of the campaign was the breakthrough of the PDs who astounded everybody by winning 14 seats. Another success story was the Workers Party, formerly Sinn Féin the Workers Party, which doubled its seat tally to four.

Haughey barely scraped into office. Although one Independent, his old arms trial associate, Neil Blaney, voted for him and another, Tony Gregory, abstained the Dáil vote on his nomination as Taoiseach. That vote ended in a tie and Haughey was only elected with the casting vote of the Ceann Comhairle, Sean Treacy. There was considerable doubt about whether his minority Government would last but Haughey proceeded to confound his critics by cutting public spending by even more than the Fine Gael led government he had denounced for the previous four years. He also implemented the Anglo-Irish Agreement he had tried to sabotage a little over a year earlier. Talk of renegotiating it was quietly forgotten and his Foreign Minister, Brian Lenihan, enthusiastically worked the institutions established under its terms. The U turn was breath taking but it was precisely what the country needed.

Haughey's successful policy on public spending cuts was only possible because of the role played by two important political figures. One was the Minister for Finance, Ray MacSharry. A tough politician from Sligo with tunnel vision, he was the only member of the cabinet not in the least intimidated by 'the Boss'. In the same job in 1982 he had accepted the Department of Finance diagnosis for Ireland's economic woes in 'The Way Forward' and in 1987 he set about implementing it, come hell or high water.

The other politician who deserved a huge amount of credit for Ireland's economic recovery was the new Fine Gael leader, Alan Dukes, who put country before party and backed the Fianna Fáil Government's economic policies. FitzGerald had stepped down as party leader immediately after the election and was replaced by Dukes who defeated two rivals, John Bruton and Peter Barry, to win the leadership. Dukes had a meteoric rise through the political world in the 1980s. First elected in 1981, he was appointed Minister for Agriculture on his first day in the Dáil and was Minister for Finance for most of the period between 1982 and 1987. A tall, thin figure who smoked like a chimney, Dukes was incredibly bright but did not suffer fools. When a journalist once put it to him that he was cold and arrogant Dukes replied: 'Inside this flinty exterior there beats a heart of stone.' The comment showed that he did have a sense of humour but it was not obvious to many of his colleagues.

Dukes's decision to back Haughey's strategy of public spending cuts was not welcomed by some of the more experienced politicians in the party who thought his strategy naive. However, it was a logical follow through on the policy proclaimed by FitzGerald on the night of the election, when he pledged to back the Government if it faced up to economic reality. Dukes honoured that promise by adopting what became known as the 'Tallaght strategy' which involved Fine Gael underpinning Fianna Fáil in the Dáil. The Government regularly mustered well over 120 votes in Dáil divisions on controversial subjects. It was a political experiment not seen before or since but it served the country well although it ultimately cost Dukes the party leadership.

The result was that Haughey's Government managed to slash public spending, turn the economy around and pave the way for what came to be known as 'the Celtic Tiger'. As well as cutting, Haughey also displayed imagination and flair by coming up with initiatives like the creation of the Financial Services Centre in Dublin's docklands (the IFSC) and the regeneration of Temple Bar. Both soon became symbols of a new Ireland. Although a small man, barely five foot six, Haughey always sought to impose his will on others and he had an aura about him that grew during this period in office. He achieved a lot in a very short time by demonstrating flair and ruthlessness. He was in complete command of his cabinet and was utterly decisive in his dealings with Ministers and with the Dáil.

He imposed his style at an early cabinet meeting when one Minister started to outline a problem that confronted his Department. Haughey cut him off brusquely. 'I am not interested in your problems. When you have a solution bring it to cabinet for approval,' he said. Cabinet meetings were short, rarely lasting two hours by contrast with FitzGerald whose cabinet meetings often went on all day, and sometimes into the early hours of the morning.

Haughey could be charming and brutal in equal measure. Fianna Fáil Senator, Don Lydon, a strong supporter, once irritated him during a conversation in the Taoiseach's office. Lydon was dismissed curtly from the leader's presence but, in his confusion, couldn't find the door in the wood panelled office. Haughey ignored him for a couple of minutes then looked up from his desk and barked:

'What are you still doing here?'

'I can't find the door, Taoiseach,' replied Lydon.

'Then why don't you jump out the fucking window,' snapped Haughey.

A key element in the economic turn around was an agreement with the trade unions and the other social partners to follow a policy of wage restraint, in tandem with the massive public spending cuts. The Programme for National Recovery agreed with the social partners was Haughey's pride and joy. 'A pearl of very great price' was how he described it. Haughey's cabinet favourite the Minister for Labour, Bertie Ahern, played an important role in the negotiations with the unions.

One of the downsides of the ruthless policy of spending cuts was that the health service took a hammering. This was to have an impact on society for the next two decades and became a source of continuing political controversy that is ongoing. At this stage, though, with Fine Gael backing Haughey and the

PDs usually doing the same it was only the Labour Party and small left-wing groups who put up real opposition to the policy of spending cuts.

In an effort to demonstrate some independence and avoid being out manoeuvred by the other opposition parties, Fine Gael occasionally backed private member's motions critical of the Government. This resulted in a number of Dáil defeats for Fianna Fáil but they did not impact on its ability to survive as they had no effect on Government policy. Still, they stung Haughey and, misled by high opinion poll ratings, he decided in the summer of 1989 that he could win an overall majority and govern without reliance on Fine Gael. After a Dáil defeat on a motion calling for the allocation of €500,000 to help haemophiliacs infected with the AIDS virus by tainted blood products, he called a general election to coincide with the European elections scheduled for June 1989. The move was a slap in the face for Fine Gael which had supported his economic policies but in any event it backfired badly for Haughey. The campaign was dominated by the issue of health cuts rather than the economic recovery, which still had not begun to impact on the public imagination.

Instead of winning his longed-for overall majority, which the polls had again predicted, Fianna Fáil lost 4 seats and ended up with 77. Fine Gael had a small recovery, gaining 4 seats to 55, Labour gained 3 and the PDs slumped to 6. The Workers Party made a big breakthrough winning seven seats. There was some irony in the fact that a party committed to a Marxist ideology made its big breakthrough in Ireland just as the communist world was collapsing.

The result created a stalemate in the Dáil. Haughey did not

have the numbers to be elected as Taoiseach. Neither did Dukes who had fought the election on a joint platform with the PDs. For the first time in the history of the state the Dáil failed to elect a Taoiseach when it met after a general election. The country was faced with an unprecedented political and constitutional crisis and the politicians were forced to find a way out or fight another election immediately.

Dukes could not underwrite another 'Tallaght strategy' after the way Haughey abandoned the first. Instead he proposed that Fianna Fáil and Fine Gael should form a grand coalition with himself and Haughey rotating in the Taoiseach's office with an almost equal share out of cabinet positions. This was dismissed out of hand by Fianna Fáil and was not meant to be taken seriously in any case.

The inescapable logic of the election arithmetic was that Fianna Fáil with 77 seats and the PDs with 6 should come to some form of arrangement, as their combined total came to the magic figure of 83, a bare Dáil majority. Haughey was open to an arrangement with the PDs but he strongly resisted the notion of a coalition, on the basis that this would involve the abandonment of a Fianna Fáil 'core value'. Eventually, though, Haughey realised that he had no choice and, against the wishes of some of his most important Ministers, he agreed to a coalition. Many found it incredible that Haughey and O'Malley, who royally detested each other, could put their long-standing personal differences aside to form a government. Each needed the other; Haughey wanted to retain power at all costs and O'Malley needed power to save his party, which had done very badly in the election.

In office the two professional politicians of great ability

worked well together. The PDs got their core value, tax cuts, into the programme for government and, by abandoning its notional core value of no coalition, Fianna Fáil was able to hold on to its real core value, the exercise of power. Fianna Fáil's decision to enter coalition was likened by Dick Walsh, the political editor of *The Irish Times*, to its decision to abandon abstentionism and enter Dáil Éireann 1927. Just as the decision to end abstentionism created the basis for a long period of Fianna Fáil hegemony in the 1930s and 1940s, the decision to accept coalition created the basis for Fianna Fáil rule for the following two decades.

Under the first Fianna Fáil-PD coalition from 1989 to 1992, the PD tax cutting agenda began to be implemented and the economy continued its steady improvement. However, the political world lurched from one crisis to another. There were also rumours, later confirmed, that Haughey was using his position to collect large amounts of money from wealthy benefactors. Some of his connections with the wealthy elite got him into trouble at that stage and he was forced to establish a judicial tribunal to investigate the meat industry after a string of allegations about his relationship with beef baron, Larry Goodman.

MNÁ NA HÉIREANN

The first big crisis of Haughey's last government began when the political world was set alight in 1990 by a presidential election that gave the country its first woman head of state and the first non-Fianna Fáil politician to occupy the highest office in the land. The election of Mary Robinson was a momentous event that marked a key moment in the creation of modern Ireland. Her victory reflected the huge social changes that had been taking place since the 1960s and, in particular, it was a manifestation of the changing place of women in Irish society.

Although a number of prominent women had played a role in the struggle for Independence, Irish politics was almost entirely a male preserve in the subsequent decades. This happened despite the fact that the Free State became one of the first countries in the world to give women the vote on the same basis as men. One of the reasons women faded from the political arena was that all six women TDs who were members of the Second Dáil voted against the Treaty of 1922. This had two consequences. The first was that women did not have a voice in the councils of the Free State during its formative years. The second was that the image of women in politics became associated with extremism and violence.

In the decades after the Civil War the women elected to the Dáil tended largely to be the widows or female relations of deceased TDs. They generally contributed little to Dáil debates and focused on being efficient constituency deputies. On average there were just three to five women members of each Dáil between the 1920s and the 1980s. Máire Geoghegan-Quinn of Fianna Fáil, who had succeeded to her father's seat in Galway West, became the first woman cabinet Minister in an independent Ireland in 1979. This heralded a new era for women in politics.

On taking over as leader of Fine Gael in 1977, Garret FitzGerald set out deliberately to encourage women to join the party and to stand for election. During the 1970s the Women's Political Association was established to encourage women to get involved and one of its prominent figures, Gemma Hussey, was elected as a Fine Gael TD and was appointed to the cabinet as Minister for Education by FitzGerald. She was succeeded in that post by Mary O'Rourke of Fianna Fáil. During the 1980s the number of women TDs rose into the low teens but progress remained painfully slow with relatively few women putting themselves forward for election and relatively few making it to the Dáil. Mary Robinson's candidature for the presidency changed the political landscape.

Since its creation in the 1937 Constitution the office of President had usually been occupied by senior Fianna Fáil figures coming to the close of their political careers. The first President, Douglas Hyde, a Protestant and the founder of the Gaelic League did not fit this category but he was succeeded by Sean T. O'Kelly, a prominent Fianna Fáil figure who served two seven-year terms, the second without an election. In 1959 Eamon de Valera began the first of his two terms and he only retired from office in 1973 at the age of 91. He was succeeded by the former Fianna Fáil Minister, Erskine Childers, who defeated Tom O'Higgins of Fine Gael. However, Childers died of a heart attack after a little over a year in office and was replaced by the Chief Justice, Cearbhall Ó Dálaigh, without an election. When Ó Dálaigh resigned in 1976 he was also replaced without election by Ireland's EU Commissioner Patrick Hillery. Against his will Hillery was pushed into serving a second term, again without an election.

At the beginning of 1990 the Labour leader, Dick Spring, declared his intention of forcing the first Presidential election in almost 20 years. He came up with an inspired choice; the former Labour senator, Mary Robinson, who was already an icon of liberal Ireland. Born Mary Therese Bourke in Ballina, County Mayo in 1944, Robinson was the daughter of two medical doctors. After a distinguished academic record in Trinity College Dublin she was appointed Reid Professor of Law at the college and elected by its graduates to Seanad Éireann as an Independent in 1969. She married Nicholas Robinson in 1970 but her parents refused to attend the wedding as he was a Protestant.

She joined the Labour Party in 1976 and narrowly failed to win a seat in the general election of 1977. For the next decade Robinson campaigned on a wide range of liberal issues, including the right of women to sit on juries, an end to the marriage bar on women in the civil service and, most controversially of all, the legalisation of contraception. Robinson resigned from the Labour Party in 1986 at the lack of consultation with unionists in advance of the Anglo-Irish Agreement.

Robinson made it clear that she would run as an Independent candidate, with Labour backing, rather than as a purely party candidate. She was the first woman candidate ever for the post and she started her campaign in early summer long before Fianna Fáil or Fine Gael selected their candidates for the November election. By the time the bigger parties picked their candiadtes in the autumn, the Robinson campaign had captured the imaginaton of the country, particularly of women. Her appeal to Mná na hÉireann (the women of Ireland) crossed the barriers of party, class and creed. As the election drew close it was clear Robinson was ahead of the Fine Gael candidate, Austin Currie, and closing on the Fianna Fáil nominee, veteran politician, Brian Lenihan.

Lenihan might still have had a chance of winning the election if his campaign had not run into a crisis at a critical stage. What happened was that a post-graduate student, Jim Duffy, had conducted a long interview with Lenihan earlier in the year. The release of a tape recording of the interview revealed him giving a very different account of an attempt by the Haughey Government to pressurise President Hillery in 1982 than the account he had given in public. Dukes put down a motion of no confidence in the Government, the PDs indicated that they would have difficulties supporting it as long as Lenihan remained in the cabinet and huge pressure developed on him to resign as Minister for Defence. When he refused to go, Lenihan was sacked by Haughey just a week before the election. While he still won more first preference votes than Robinson, she was elected with Fine Gael transfers. Robinson proved a remarkably popular president, taking a much higher profile than her predecessors.

Her clear vision enabled her to raise issues in a manner which did not break the tight constraints of a very limited office. She highlighted the diaspora, the vast number of Irish emigrants and people of Irish descent around the world. Robinson also helped to change the face of Anglo-Irish relations, visiting Britain and becoming the first Irish president to visit Queen Elizabeth II at Buckingham Palace. She welcomed visits by senior British royals, most notably the Prince of Wales to her residence at Áras an Uachtaráin. She left office a few months before her term had expired to become UN High Commissioner for Human Rights.

Mary Robinson was succeeded as President in November 1997 by Mary McAleese, who was also a former Reid Professor of Law at Trinity College. McAleese was the nominee of Fianna Fáil and went on to become an equally popular President getting a second term without a contest in 2003.

The number of women in the Dáil rose after Robinson's election hitting the 20 mark for the first time in 1992 and again in the 1997 election, and in 2002 the number crept up to 22. Instead of 'a woman' being appointed to cabinet, as was the practice in the 1980s, women have more recently been apppointed on merit. The second Ahern Government had 3 women cabinet Ministers out of 15 – Mary Harney being the first women to become a party leader and to hold the office of Tánaiste.

GOLDEN CIRCLES

If Fianna Fáil was shocked at the Robinson victory, Fine Gael was shattered by the slump in its vote to just 17% of the first preference total. Dukes was blamed by some for picking the wrong candidate and by others for contesting the election at all. His personal style had alienated most of his front bench colleagues who regarded him as too remote and condescending. When a motion of no confidence was put down by the former party whip, Fergus O'Brien, his leadership was doomed. After putting up a fight for a few days Dukes realised that a majority of the parliamentary party were against him so he stepped down and was replaced by his deputy leader, John Bruton.

Meanwhile, the Haughey roller coaster continued through 1991 with further controversies and claims about golden circles of influence. Many of the people who had put him in the Taoiseach's office in December 1979, decided that it was time for him to go. Two of his chief lieutenants, Albert Reynolds and Padraig Flynn, led the fourth heave against his leadership in November 1991, but Haughey survived their revolt, just as he had survived O'Malley's efforts to oust him almost a decade earlier. However, in January 1992, the past caught up with him when the former Minister for Justice, Sean Doherty, claimed Haughey had known about his decision to tap the phones of political journalists, Geraldine Kennedy and Bruce Arnold. Despite their reservations about the people trying to oust Haughey the PDs had no choice but to give him the same ultimatum they applied to Lenihan. Haughey saw the game was up and he bowed out.

Albert Reynolds became the new Taoiseach – managing to do a deal with Haughey's protégé, Bertie Ahern. The 59-year-old Reynolds, a successful businessman from Longford who made his fortune from ballrooms during the showband boom of the 1960s, was a no nonsense risk taker and dealer. Sean Duignan, the RTÉ broadcaster, who became his Government press secretary, had his first lengthy conversation with Reynolds around this time. He could not help being attracted by the direct uncomplicated style of the Longford man: 'I found his breezy blend of small town mateyness and "up she flew" optimism appealing. Here was one of my own western breed who made no apologies for his background or the kind of grafting he had to do to climb to the top. "Keep 'er going Patsy and fuck the begrudgers".'

Reynolds had served in various economic Ministries, ending up in Finance, after the departure of Ray MacSharry to Brussels as EU Commissioner in 1989. He was fired by Haughey for his revolt in 1991 but immediately became the leader in waiting.

When Haughey was forced to resign he encouraged Bertie Ahern to take on Reynolds and it appeared there was going to be a contest. However, after a weekend of ringing around, Ahern concluded that he did not have the numbers to win so he did a deal with Reynolds and withdrew from the race. Reynolds was the unanimous choice of the parliamentary party and Ahern became the Minister for Finance. Over 15 years later it was revealed that he had accepted between €50,000 and €100,000 from wealthy business friends in Dublin and Manchester while he held this office.

Reynolds astonished everybody by announcing on the day of his election as Taoiseach that his priority was to settle the Northern Ireland issue once and for all. He had never said much about the North in public but, characteristically, he abandoned all discretion and protocols in his search for a deal. It had been conventional wisdom that a political solution was a prerequisite to ending violence. Reynolds simply reversed the priorities by saying that peace was necessary before a solution could be found. He encouraged John Hume to continue talking to Sinn Féin leader, Gerry Adams, he engaged in intensive contacts with Fr Alex Reid, the Belfast based Redemptorist priest who had huge influence with leading republicans. The other prong of Reynolds's strategy was to convince the British Prime Minister, John Major, to engage in the dialogue with republicans. Reynolds and Major had become friends during their Finance Ministry days and their personal chemistry enabled them to look at the North and Anglo-Irish relations in a new light. They did have ferocious rows at times but the combined efforts of Reynolds, Major, Hume and Adams transformed the situation.

Reynolds was often reckless in his search for peace but his unorthodox approach worked. However, the same recklessness destroyed the two Governments he led and put a premature end to his time at the top. When he took the reins of power in February 1992, Fianna Fáil was in coalition with the PDs, a position described by Reynolds as 'a temporary little arrangement.' He made his hostility to the PDs clear at every turn and the coalition collapsed in November of that year when the antagonism between himself and O'Malley spilled over at the Beef Tribunal, established after allegations about Larry Goodman's role in the industry. Reynolds called O'Malley 'dishonest' and the coalition fell apart.

Tension between the parties was fuelled by a serious controversy over abortion in 1992. What became known as 'the X case' involved a decision by the Attorney General, Harry Whelehan, to refuse to allow a minor, who had become pregnant as the result of sexual abuse, to travel to Britain for an abortion. Reynolds proposed an amendment to the constitutional ban on abortion that would affirm the right of an individual to travel and to receive information. The third prong of the amendment was a redefinition of the abortion ban itself, which was attacked by liberals, including the PDs, as being too restrictive and by conservatives for being too broad. The abortion referendums and the general election were held on the same day, 25 November 1992. Reynolds had a disastrous general election because many voters could not understand why the Government had broken up. He was blamed for precipitating an unnecessarily early election and the Fianna Fáil campaign quickly turned into a shambles. John Bruton and Fine Gael fared little better as the party was not seen as a viable alternative Government. The star of the campaign was Labour leader, Dick Spring. He had developed into a superb Dáil performer and when he staked a claim to the Taoiseach's office as the price of any coalition Labour would be involved with after the election his party's campaign took off. Opinion polls showed Spring as the favoured choice for Taoiseach with Labour passing out Fine Gael.

When the votes were counted Fianna Fáil had slumped to its lowest share of the vote since 1927, dropping 5% to 39% and winning just 68 Dáil seats. Fine Gael did equally badly. The party also dropped 5% and lost 10 seats to end up with 45. Labour won just over 19% of the vote and 33 seats, by far the best performance in the party's history. The PDs surprised a lot of people by gaining 4 seats to 10 while the Workers Party (now rebranded as the Democratic Left) lost 3 and came back with just 4. In the three referendums held on the same day the two non-controversial amendments were carried but the substantial one on abortion was lost.

Reynolds was shattered by the result but quickly realised that all was not lost. While most of the early post election speculation in the media centred on the prospect of a rainbow Government involving Fine Gael, Labour and DL that option had two things going against it. The first was that Bruton and Spring had a very poor relationship due to their rows in cabinet during the 1980s. The second was that Bruton had ruled out involving the DL and the third was that the potential rainbow was a seat short in any case.

That created an opportunity for Reynolds, who seized it with both hands. He had instructed his advisors to prepare a policy document for a potential deal with Labour. When the rainbow talks collapsed and Spring announced that he was open to talks with Fianna Fáil he was immediately presented with a document that included all main objectives. As in its negotiations with the PDs in 1989, Fianna Fáil was prepared to let its coalition partner dictate the programme for Government as long as it held on to power.

Spring found the offer irresistible and entered the first Fianna Fáil-Labour coalition. Spring became Tánaiste and Minister for Foreign Affairs and brought five colleagues into the cabinet but Reynolds could hardly believe his luck to be back as Taoiseach after the terrible election result. Spring's decision to enter coalition with Fianna Fáil, after waging such a successful election campaign against the party, distressed many Labour supporters.

One of the reasons Spring found the prospect of power so attractive was that Reynolds had told him about the early stirrings of the peace process. On top of that Reynolds negotiated an €8 billion package of EU aid for Ireland at a summit meeting held just after the election. With historic progress on the North and the economy in prospect Spring wanted to be in on the action.

Reynolds and Spring worked well on the peace process. Reynolds built on the good personal relationship he had forged with John Major. Work on what became known as the Joint Declaration between the two Governments went on through 1993. In the background the republican movement was being consulted to establish if a wording could be found that would encourage them to end their campaign of violence and fully commit to the political process.

The talks between the prime ministers came to a head at a

special Anglo-Irish summit in Dublin Castle in December 1993. A fierce row developed between Reynolds and Major when the British proposed yet another new draft of the Declaration rather than the working text that had been painfully put together by officials from both sides. 'You are trying to make a fool out of me, John, and I won't have it. We'll not do business on the basis of this,' said Reynolds throwing the British draft into the middle of the table during a meeting of the leaders and their respective delegations. Reynolds used a couple of swear words that so stunned Major, he snapped a pencil he was holding in half. Major suggested a private meeting and the pair retired to an anteroom. When they emerged after half an hour they both looked pale.

'How did it go, Taoiseach?' asked Dick Spring's advisor, Fergus Finlay.

'It wasn't too bad. He chewed the bollix off me but I took a few lumps out of him,' replied Reynolds.

Just a little over a week later on 15 December, Reynolds and Major signed the Joint Declaration in the cabinet room at Downing Street. It was the same room in which Michael Collins and Arthur Griffith had signed the Anglo-Irish Treaty in 1922. It was a truly historic occasion that paved the way for the IRA ceasefire and the Good Friday Agreement. It would never have happened without the drive and bravado of Albert Reynolds and the patience and intelligence of John Major. 'The great point about my relationship with Albert Reynolds was that we liked one another and could have a row without giving up on each other. The air was clearer when we left the room,' recorded Major in his memoirs.

Although Reynolds established a relationship of trust with Major he never managed the same with his Labour Tánaiste even though the Labour and Fianna Fáil Ministers bonded well and an unexpected rapport developed between the two sides. A big problem for Labour was that many of the party supporters were shocked at the decision to coalesce with Fianna Fáil after the years Spring had spent attacking the party. The party was put on the rack by the media and opposition every time an 'ethical' issue involving Fianna Fáil came on to the political agenda. Despite progress on the economy and the North the partnership between Reynolds and Spring fell apart in less than two years. A claim by Reynolds that he was 'vindicated' by the Beef Tribunal report almost brought the coalition down and it was only saved because the IRA cessation followed within days and Spring felt he could not pull out of Government at such a critical time.

Another disagreement followed, however, this time over Reynolds's determination to make his Attorney General, Harry Whelehan, president of the High Court. The ingredient that destroyed the coalition was the revelation that a warrant for a paedophile priest, Brendan Smyth, had not been processed by the Attorney's General's office. Whelehan had no involvement of any kind in the episode, which appears to have been due simply to an administrative error, but it was the straw that broke the camel's back.

The collapse of the Reynolds Government was one of the most sensational episodes in the history of the Dáil and what made it all the more dramatic was that the key debates were broadcast live on television. One of the critical elements in the drama was that the balance of power in the Dáil had changed since 1992 as a result of by-election wins by Fine Gael and Democratic Left. An alternative coalition was now possible if Labour switched sides in the Dáil and that is precisely what Spring did. He negotiated a deal for Government with Fine Gael and DL and John Bruton took over as Taoiseach without a general election taken place. It was the only time in the history of the state that a change of government happened in this way.

One of the reasons the Dáil sorted out the mess without a general election was a belief among the political parties that President Robinson would exercise the right of the president to refuse Reynolds a dissolution of the Dáil, as he no longer had a majority in the House. This prerogative had never been exercised and although President Robinson was never ultimately presented with the choice it was a major factor prompting Reynolds to resign from office instead of going to the country. Bertie Ahern replaced Reynolds as leader, he was considered a popular figure in the country who had good relations with his Labour colleagues and, more importantly, was very popular with the public. Fianna Fáil switched leaders on the basis that it would enable the party to continue in Government and initially it seemed as if the strategy would work. However, with just 24 hours to go before signing a deal with the new Fianna Fáil leader, Dick Spring decided he could not take the risk and instead he opted to do a deal with Fine Gael.

CHAPTER ELEVEN

FROM THE RAINBOW TO AHERN

John Bruton got his chance of being Taoiseach in an unexpected fashion but he confounded his critics by the competent manner he exercised power. A TD since 1969, Bruton was a formidable conviction politician. At cabinet in the 1980s he had given vent to his frustration with Labour's refusal to face up to the need for public spending cuts and made some enemies as a result. He was twice Minister for Finance in dreadfully difficult circumstances in 1981/82 and 1986/87. During both short stints he brought forward budgets that precipitated general elections; the first was an accident but the second was carefully planned. Both budgets showed a commitment to getting to grips with the problems facing the country rather than shirking them as most politicians would have done. While he acted courageously his image suffered and he got the reputation of being difficult to work with.

On the North he also had unambiguous views. A fierce critic of IRA terrorism, he had no sympathy for Sinn Féin and was impatient with politicians and officials who pandered to that party's agenda during the 1990s. Bruton, who came from a comfortable farming family in Meath, was very conscious of his family's political roots in the Centre Party of the 1930s, which in turn was a successor of the old Irish Parliamentary Party. He came from the Dillon wing of Fine Gael rather than the Michael Collins wing and that created its own tensions in the party. As Taoiseach he adorned walls of his office with the pictures of two politicians. One was of John Redmond and the other was Seán Lemass. That choice said a lot about Bruton's vision of the future and the past.

Under Bruton the economic recovery began to accelerate. Labour had insisted on taking Finance and the party's first occupant of that portfolio, Ruairi Quinn, proved to be a highly competent Minister and brought in the first budget surplus in decades. Bruton surprised people by running his three-handed coalition smoothly and there were no ideological rows, as in the 1980s, primarily because times were better. The Taoiseach also struck up an unlikely bond with DL leader, Proinsias De Rossa, whom he had refused to contemplate going into government with two years earlier.

One major issue facing the Government was a commitment to hold another divorce referendum. Although he was a devout Catholic and came from the more conservative wing of his party, Bruton led the campaign with courage and when it seemed to be slipping to defeat in the final days he delivered an impassioned speech that helped carry it across the line. It was the closest referendum result in the history of the state with 50.2% voting Yes and 49.8% voting No.

On the North, Bruton tried to maintain continuity and devoted a lot of time and effort to the negotiation of the Frameworks document of 1995 that set out the basis for devolution and cross-border institutions. Still, as a long time critic of the republican movement he could not disguise his impatience with republican foot dragging after the IRA cessation. He could not see why much quicker progress could not be made to full decommissioning and a winding down of the IRA. By contrast unionists regarded Bruton as the first Taoiseach to understand their position and, while that did not earn him much credit with vocal nationalists, it kept the process inching forward. He welcomed the heir to the British throne, Prince Charles, at a state dinner in Dublin Castle which symbolised the new relationship between Ireland and Britain.

The big issue at this stage was the insistence of the British that the IRA would have to decommission its weapons before it could talk to Sinn Féin directly. In 1996 the republicans abandoned their ceasefire and bombed London again in order to push the Government into backing down on the issue. The Canary wharf bomb, which killed two people and caused hundreds of millions of pounds worth of damage to property, came as a shock to both Governments and though it was in reality a bargaining tool rather than a full-scale return to violence, that was not apparent at the time.

Bruton was pressurised by Labour into calling a general election for June 1997, although he would have preferred to wait until the autumn. A reason for waiting was the growing embarrassment to Fianna Fáil at the first of a series of judicial tribunals into political corruption. The issue had initially come as an embarrassment to Bruton because it started with the revelation that his Minister for Public Enterprise, Michael Lowry, had the bill for extensive renovations on his house paid for by the supermarket tycoon, Ben Dunne. Lowry resigned within 24 hours of the story breaking – but it represented just the first in a series of disclosures about payments to politicians. The information about Lowry had leaked from court documents concerning a row in the Dunne family. Further leaks indicated that Ben Dunne had paid substantial sums of money to Haughey. The McCracken tribunal set up to investigate the payments to Lowry and Haughey was on course to finish by the summer of 1997 and its findings were bound to be an embarrassment to Fianna Fáil.

Despite this Labour pressed for an election before the summer. Spring and his Ministers were tired after almost five years in Government and could not face the pressure of waiting until the autumn. It was a fatal miscalculation. The three-party rainbow went into the campaign against a rival coalition made up of Fianna Fáil and the PDs. Bruton's rival for the Taoiseach's office was the popular, Bertie Ahern, who had succeeded Albert Reynolds as Fianna Fáil leader in December 1994, and at the age of 42 had become the youngest ever leader of his party.

Ahern was always something of a paradox. He was a politician who craved public approval and got it; opinion polls from the late 1980s onwards consistently showed him as the most popular politician in the country. Elected a TD at the age of 25 in 1977 he built up a strong political base in Dublin Central, surrounding himself with a coterie of friends and associates who would remain close to him for the rest of his political life. He was a Haughey man from the beginning and helped the 'Boss' by undermining the electoral base of his constituency colleague George Colley.

As Haughey's chief whip during the early 1980s and later Minister for Labour, Ahern made a good public impression by remaining calm and courteous even in the most difficult of circumstances. He became one of Haughey's inner circle, so much so that he was made a co-signatory on the controversial party leader's bank account in 1982 until Haughey left office. Despite his popularity both parliamentary colleagues and journalists never knew him as well as Reynolds or even

Haughey. He never mingled much in the Dáil, preferring the company of his friends in Drumcondra, who formed a formidable political organisation dedicated to his interests. People found it difficult to get behind the mask but in the constituency his political opponents both inside and outside Fianna Fáil found him to be a ruthless operator. He built up a powerful and exceptionally well-funded organisation in Dublin and even acquired a permanent headquarters in Drumcondra, which is located in a large red-brick house called St Luke's.

Although he is a devout Catholic and unashamedly wears ash on his forehead every Ash Wednesday, Ahern has a complicated private life. His marriage broke up in 1987. He later became involved in a relationship with a Fianna Fáil activist, Celia Larkin, who went to work for him as his constituency secretary in the Department of Labour and subsequently became his special advisor in the Department of the Taoiseach. The relationship was a very public one but it ended in 2003. Larkin was very involved in developing Ahern's constituency organisation and the running costs of St Luke's that is funded by an annual dinner in the Royal Hospital Kilmainham. Since he became a Minister in 1987 the prominent businesses in Dublin Central and beyond have been invited to buy tickets for the dinner. This enabled Ahern to run the full-time constituency office and to spend considerable amounts of money at election time. He estimated his expenditure on the 1989 election as around £20,000 and the 1992 election at around £30,000. Haughey once remarked of Ahern: 'He's the best, the most cunning, the most devious of them all.'

The PDs also had a new leader: Mary Harney replaced Des

O'Malley after he stepped down as leader in October 1993. A widely respected figure, even among people who rejected the economic analysis of the PDs, Harney was first woman to be elected leader of a political party in Ireland. She had shown her mettle as a politician by having the courage to leave Fianna Fáil over the party's Northern policy and, in all likelihood, the PDs would never have been formed without her prompting of O'Malley. Harney was Minister for Environmental Protection in the Fianna Fáil-PD government of 1989 and introduced a ban on the sale of coal that put an end to the problem of severe smog in Dublin. She was the logical successor as party leader but first had to see off the challenge of the party's former general secretary, Pat Cox, who had got elected to the Dáil in 1992 after winning a seat for the PDs in the 1989 European elections. Harney won the contest with ease but then endured a series of tribulations. The worst was the defection of Cox from the party and his successful challenge for a European seat as an Independent at the expense of O'Malley.

Harney saw that the only way the PDs could achieve power in 1997 was in coalition with Fianna Fáil and the parties came together in the election campaign with joint policies that committed them to reducing personal income tax rates. The rainbow parties sought a mandate for a more complicated reform of the tax system favouring lower income earners.

The election was hard fought. Fianna Fáil did well but so did Fine Gael. Labour was cut in half but so were the PDs. Fianna Fáil won 39% of the first preference vote, the same share as 1992, but increased its number of seats by 8 to 77, the PDs had a disastrous election and dropped from 10 seats in 1992 to just 4, Fine Gael did well, pushing back up from 41 to 54, but

Labour was almost cut in half both in terms of votes and seats and ended up with just 17. The DL came back with four, the Greens went up from one to two, Sinn Féin took one, the Socialist Party one and there were six Others.

The result was close but Fianna Fáil and the PDs between them had 81 seats. Ahern was elected Taoiseach with the support of three Independents and the second Fianna Fáil-PD coalition was in business. While it had many rocky moments in its first year in office the Ahern-Harney Government proved remarkable solid and was still in power a decade later. The equable temperament of both party leaders was important for stability but the glue that held the coalition together was the Minister for Finance, Charlie McCreevy. A long time friend of Harney's he had been involved in the manoeuvres that led to the founding of the PDs in 1985 and only pulled back at the last moment. He shared the PD belief that lower taxes were a vital component of a vibrant economy. Income tax rates were quickly lowered and so were corporate and capital taxes. The result was that an already growing economy was propelled into a decade long boom. The era of the Celtic Tiger had dawned with sensational economic growth rates transforming the country.

On Northern Ireland too, there was also remarkable progress. The arrival of Fianna Fáil in Government prompted the IRA to resume its ceasefire. Ahern established a quick rapport with the new British Prime Minister, Tony Blair, and the result was the Good Friday Agreement of 1998 – which heralded a new era in Anglo-Irish relations. The Agreement was based on the so-called three-stranded approach to a settlement long advocated by John Hume. The first strand involved a power sharing arrangement in the North between unionists and nationalists; the second covered North-South relations and the third strand the east-west relationship between the Irish Republic and the UK. The Agreement was ratified by the people of Ireland in simultaneous referendums North and South. Part of the deal was that the territorial claim to the North contained in Articles 2 and 3 of the Irish constitution was dropped.

After the euphoria of the referendums being passed – problems developed. Strand one was the thorny issue and while a power-sharing executive involving all the main parties including Sinn Féin, was set up it ultimately collapsed. Still, there was no return to violence and the IRA eventually decommissioned its arsenal, five years after the original deadline. The other relationships improved steadily and the Irish and British Governments were completely united in their approach to the problem. In the autumn of 2006, the Governments gave the Northern parties an ultimatum to either work the power sharing arrangements or have the region run from outside.

At a meeting involving both Governments and all the Northern parties at St Andrews in Scotland in the autumn of 2006 yet another formula was devised for the establishment of a devolved Executive, with a new deadline being set for March 2007. The deal involved Sinn Fein's acceptance of the policing arrangements for Northern Ireland, to be followed by DUP acceptance of power sharing. Assembly elections were scheduled for early March with the first meeting to take place on 26 March.

Ahern laid great store at the success of his Northern policy and devoted an enormous amount of time and attention to it. Despite the hiccups along the way the policy was a resounding success. Relations between Ireland and Britain were placed on a better footing than at any time since Independence in 1922 as the two countries settled into a healthy neighbourly relationship. The IRA ceasefire, declared immediately after Ahern became Taoiseach, held for a decade and became irreversible and, even if there were difficulties about the creation of a power-sharing arrangement within Northern Ireland, poor inter-community relationships in the region no longer had the ability to poison the relationship between the people of the two islands.

The success of his Northern policy reflected considerable success on Ahern, and Fianna Fáil supporters were proud of the fact that relations between Ireland and Britain had never been better. It could be argued, of course, that it was precisely because Fianna Fáil had come to accept the validity of the consent principle, something that been accepted by most other parties long before, that the new era in Anglo-Irish relations became possible. Ahern's decision to support the amendment of Articles 2 and 3 of the Constitution removed the territorial claim on the North and with it the foundation stone of de Valera's Northern policy.

On the negative side there were shocking revelations about the level of corruption that flourished during the Haughey era during the early days of Ahern's government. A series of judicial tribunals established that Haughey had received over £11.5 million (over €30 million in 2007 terms) in 'donations' from business people. Ray Burke, the Minister for Foreign Affairs in Ahern's Government, had to resign within months of taking office because of an emerging scandal about payments made to him. He ultimately went to jail for tax offences. Another Fianna Fáil TD, Liam Lawlor, also went to jail for contempt of court but the evidence showed that he was involved in a massive scam involving the re-zoning of land around Dublin. He subsequently died in a car accident in Moscow in 2006. These scandals threatened to scupper Ahern's coalition in its early days.

Ahern himself had his problems with the Moriarty tribunal, particularly in relation to the fact that he had been a co-signatory on the controversial party leader's bank account. Ahern was initially a signatory because of his position of chief whip but his name remained on it for five years after he left that post in 1987 until Haughey finally departed the leadership. Cheques from that account signed by Ahern ended up in Haughey's personal accounts while others went to buy Charvet shirts and pay for meals at Le Coq Hardi in Ballsbridge. Questioned by the Moriarty tribunal in 1999 about how his name came to be on cheques used for such unorthodox purposes he said it was the practice to sign blank cheques which were completed by the party leader.

The first Moriarty report, which was finally published in December 2006, six months after Haughey's death, painted a shocking picture of corruption during his time at the top. It found that the scale and secretive nature of the payments to him could 'only be said to have devalued the quality of a modern democracy.' The tribunal also referred to the involvement of Ahern in signing cheques from the party leader's account that facilitated Haughey's lavish lifestyle.

While the tribunal is satisfied that Mr Ahern had no reason

to believe that the account was operated otherwise than for a proper purpose, the practice of pre-signing cheques by Mr Ahern undoubtedly facilitated the misuse of the account by Mr Haughey. This is a practice which has to be viewed as both inappropriate and imprudent.

The Opposition hoped that Ahern would be damaged by the revelations but they had no effect on his popularity. Dubbed the 'Teflon Taoiseach' he was given a virtual blank cheque of his own by the public whose affection for him remained undiminished. In any case most voters became bored with the tribunal revelations because they took so long to emerge and cost so much. The enormous fees paid to rich lawyers caused at least as much public outrage as the sins of the politicians. In any case after the disclosures about Haughey almost everything paled into insignificance. The tribunals did not have a direct impact on party politics but they had corrosive long-term influence on the electorate's esteem of politicians.

As the economic boom continued and prosperity rippled across the country Ahern's position was consolidated. It was the Opposition rather than the Government which was under pressure, as a succession of polls showed Fine Gael languishing around 20% and Bruton's satisfaction rating falling. Bruton saw off one motion of no confidence before internal dissent erupted again in the autumn of 2001 and he lost a vote of no confidence after 11 years as party leader. It was a decision – born out of desperation – that most in Fine Gael would bitterly regret. The tough talking, Michael Noonan from Limerick, who had become Bruton's leading opponent defeated Enda Kenny for the leadership and the party hoped for better days. The problem was that changing leaders was not the answer to Fine Gael's underlying problems and in fact only made them worse.

Noonan had been a successful Minister for Justice in the 1980s and despite his differences with Bruton had been brought into the rainbow Government as Minister for Health. A witty and tough talking politician from Limerick, Noonan was not short of intelligence but he conveyed a harsh and uncompromising image by comparison with the wily Ahern. His period as leader proved a searing experience for Noonan because of his handling, while Minster for Health of a controversy over people, mainly women, who had become infected with the hepatitis C virus from blood transfusions. Noonan established a compensation tribunal which actually provided far more generous awards than people in similar circumstances in other countries received. However, he became embroiled in a controversy with the victim's group and he was unfairly portrayed by the Opposition and much of the media as heartless. It was an image that stuck.

The Labour leadership changed in the aftermath of the presidential election of 1997 when Dick Spring stepped down after 15 years in the job. He was replaced by Ruairi Quinn, who had enhanced his reputation in Finance. Quinn was a product of the radical ferment that had swept through Irish universities in the late 1960s and his first foray into politics was in the so-called Gentle Revolution in UCD in 1968. After qualifying as an architect he was elected to the Dáil in 1977 for Dublin South East. He served as a cabinet Minister in the FitzGerald government of the 1980s and in the Fianna Fáil-Labour coalition of the 1990s.

As his first priority Quinn set about 'merger' talks with the Democratic Left, who had had a disappointing election in 1997, and were still struggling to come to terms with the collapse of communism. The party had lost momentum after its long journey from Sinn Fein in the 1960s, through Sinn Fein the Workers Party, and on to the Workers Party and then Democratic Left. The experience of working with Labour in the rainbow government had removed the suspicion between the two parties and the logic of a merger was obvious to both. A deal was done and Quinn expressed the hope that the 'merger' would create a new Labour Party which would have greater public appeal than the sum of its parts.

Ahern stayed in office for the full five years, in defiance of political tradition, which dictated that an election should be called some time before the end and he did not go to the country until May 2002. It was one of the strangest elections in Irish political history because it never turned into a real contest between Government and the Opposition. One of the reasons for that was that there was no alternative Government on offer as Labour took a decision not to join in a pre-election pact with a weak Fine Gael. In the months before the election as the PDs languished in the polls it became accepted political wisdom that the next Government was likely to be a coalition between Fianna Fáil and Labour.

When the Taoiseach dissolved the Dáil on 25 April 2002, all the omens were Fianna Fáil was on course for a good result but that the PDs were going to be wiped out. 'It's showtime,' declared the Fianna Fáil director of elections, PJ Mara, at the party's manifesto launch, reflecting the party's buoyant mood. At that same press conference Bertie Ahern and Charlie

McCreevy stoutly maintained that no spending cuts, secret or otherwise were being planned. It was a pledge that worked wonderfully as a campaign tactic but had long-term negative consequences for the Government.

Fianna Fáil and the PDs certainly had plenty to boast about going into the election campaign. The Irish economy had outperformed all others in the developed world for the previous five years with growth of close to 10% per annum. Unemployment had fallen from 10% to just 4% while the debt/GDP ratio was down below 35%. Income tax had been cut from 26% to 20% on the basic rate and 48% to 42% at the higher rate, capital gains tax had been halved and corporation tax slashed to 12.5%. It was an astonishing record to go to the country on.

The first national opinion polls of the campaign showed Fianna Fáil storming to victory, and although they grossly overestimated the strength of the party vote, just as in every other election back to 1987, the polls dictated the nature of the campaign. With no prospect of an alternative Government the Fine Gael campaign was crippled from the start. Noonan failed to click with the voters. His cause was not helped by a succession of opinion polls that overstated Fianna Fáil support and understated Fine Gael. Labour waged a more confident campaign but it failed to capitalise on Fine Gael weakness as voters were unclear about its post-election intentions.

The fundamental problem for the Opposition was that the economy had never been in better condition. While there had been some slowdown going into 2002 the Irish people never had it so good and the voters had no desire to rock the boat. That conferred a huge advantage on the Government parties.

After the first week of the campaign the question became not whether Fianna Fáil and the PDs would have the numbers to form a Government, but whether Fianna Fáil would have the numbers on its own. The PDs concluded that Fianna Fáil was steaming to a potential landslide and in response Michael McDowell came up with a publicity stunt that changed the course of the campaign. He climbed a lamppost near his home in Ranelagh to stick up a poster with the message, 'One-Party Government? NO thanks.' There was huge media coverage of the event and it dominated the RTÉ television news and the front pages of the following day's newspapers. The poster had a huge influence on the campaign as it focused debate in the final week on the issue of whether Fianna Fáil would be in Government on its own or with the PDs.

In the event Bertie Ahern and Fianna Fáil came tantalisingly close to the first overall majority since 1977. The party's share of the vote went up from 39% to 41% and its number of seats rose from 77 to 81. The PDs confounded the prophets of doom who had written them off, yet again. The party doubled its seat total from four to eight and effectively deprived Fianna Fáil of an overall majority. The election was a disaster for Fine Gael which lost 23 seats to end up with just 31 and Labour did poorly simply holding on to its 21 seats.

The election also marked a breakthrough for two small parties who had been steadily building a presence in the Dáil. The Greens won their first seat in the Dáil in 1989 and had pushed that figure up two in 1997. The 2002 result market a real breakthrough with the party winning six seats with 4% of the national vote, the same share as the PDs. The Fine Gael slump helped the Greens but the breakthrough created the potential for real growth in the future.

The other party to break through in 2002 was Sinn Féin. Since the rise of Fianna Fáil the party had occasionally done well. In 1957 Sinn Féin won four seats but as the elected TDs refused to recognise the Dáil the party never became a real political force. In 1985 Sinn Féin dropped abstentionism as a principle. As the peace process developed in the 1990s the party made significant inroads in the North and developed a base in the Republic. Caoimhghín Ó Caoláin became the first Sinn Féin TD to take his seat in the Dáil in 1997. In the Northern Assembly elections held in 1998 after the Good Friday Agreement, Sinn Féin won 18 seats in the 108 member chamber, just 6 behind the SDLP which had 24. In the Assembly elections of 2003 the position was reversed with Sinn Féin winning 24 and becoming the biggest nationalist party in the North for the first time.

Sinn Féin put a huge effort into the 2002 election in the Republic and managed to win 6.5% of the national vote. That translated into five seats, which was less than the Greens, and the PDs won on a smaller share of the first preference vote, but it indicated that the party had arrived as a political force in both parts of the island. Sinn Féin poured resources into establishing a presence in the more deprived areas of Dublin and in the border constituencies where they worked at grass roots level to build a political base.

Fianna Fáil and the PDs quickly negotiated their second programme for Government. The PDs got two seats at the cabinet table, instead of one, with Michael

McDowell coming in as Minister for Justice and Mary Harney remaining at Enterprise. Ahern made only minor changes to the Fianna Fáil team and the Government continued on as before.

Fine Gael after its traumatic loss of almost half its Dáil seats elected a new leader. Enda Kenny defeated Richard Bruton for the position and the then set about trying to rebuild his shattered party. The demise of Fine Gael was widely forecast in 2002 but Kenny was made of sterner stuff than many imagined and he set about his task methodically. Kenny was the same age as Ahern but had actually been elected to the Dáil a couple of years earlier in a by-election caused by the death of his father. From Mayo, the gregarious Kenny was more down to earth than other leading Fine Gael figures of recent decades and was often underestimated. Labour also changed leaders as Quinn followed the example of Noonan and stood down. The new Labour leader was elected by the members, the first time there had been a contest under new rules introduced during the Spring era, not by the parliamentarians as in Fine Gael. There was some surprise when the former Workers Party and DL TD, Pat Rabbitte, beat Brendan Howlin from 'old' Labour for the position. During the 2002 election Rabbitte had declared his unwillingness to serve in a Fianna Fáil-Labour Government and his anti-Fianna Fáil stance struck a chord with the party members around the country.

Rabbitte was from Mayo, like Kenny but had a different introduction to politics. He first became prominent in student politics in the 1970s and was a member of the Labour Party. He became a trade union official after university and became involved with Sinn Féin the Workers Party. He built up a base in his home area of Tallaght and was elected to the Dáil for Dublin South West in 1989.

Fianna Fáil's standing took a dive after the 2002 election when contrary to its election assurances cuts in public spending did prove necessary. While the cuts were a short term and necessary response to world economic downturn the voters felt betrayed. In the European and local elections of 2004 the Government took a hammering and Fine Gael came storming back, winning more seats in the European Parliament than Fianna Fáil for the first time ever and almost pulling level in terms of council seats. The resurrection of Fine Gael and a good performance by Labour prompted Kenny and Rabbitte to announce the 'Mullingar Accord' between the parties. They made it clear they would fight the next general election as a team, offering the country an alternative Government.

Ahern moved to adapt in the wake of the 2004 setback. McCreevy was dispatched to Brussels as Ireland's EU Commissioner and Brian Cowen was appointed to Finance. A hugely popular figure with his Dáil colleagues Cowen was a protégé of Albert Reynolds who gave him his first taste of cabinet experience at the age of 32. There was less emphasis in tax cutting and more on social solidarity. In the same reshuffle Harney took over Health and set about trying to reform a creaking system that had become a huge negative for the Government. As economic growth resumed after the blip of 2003 the Government's confidence was restored. In the autumn of 2006 a political crisis erupted when *The Irish Times* revealed that Ahern had accepted between €50,000 and €100,000 from business friends for his own personal use when he was Minister for Finance in 1993/94. The Taoiseach gave a long television interview in which he said he had taken the money to deal with personal problems arising from the breakdown of his marriage. The first opinion poll after controversy revealed a big jump in Fianna Fáil support and increased satisfaction with Ahern. It demonstrated that the party's hold on power was going to be very difficult to shake.

By 2006 Ahern had become the longest-serving Taoiseach since de Valera, although the county he presided over would have been unrecognisable to the Chief. Ahern's pragmatic and conciliatory style took much of the heat out of political debate and reflected the growing maturity of Irish democracy. Increasing wealth, a massive influx of workers from Eastern Europe after the enlargement of the EU in 2004 and a long construction boom transformed Ireland from one of the poorest to one of the richest nations in Europe.

Despite the country's new found wealth, the Government appeared unable to sort out the problems in the Health service and it also responded slowly to the need for major infrastructural investment. Sky rocketing house prices and long commuting times were also a source of discontent and while most people were financially better off then ever before relative poverty increased from 1997 to 2007.

By 2006 the population of the Republic had risen to 4.2 million and the dark days of the late 1950s, when the numbers had dropped to 2.8 million, seemed as far away as the Famine. If the first 40 years of Irish independence proved a disappointment, the prosperous country of 2007 was the ultimate vindication of the Lemass-Whitaker strategy. How that prosperity can be developed to create a truly fair society in the future will be the test of today's politicians.

BIBLIOGRAPHY

This short bibliography lists the essential reference works on which the book is based and also some of the general histories and biographies consulted by the author.

Reference books:

Boylan, Henry, *A Dictionary of Irish Biography*, G&M, Dublin, 1998.

Connolly, SJ (ed.), *The Oxford Companion to Irish History*, OUP, Oxford, 1998.

Donnelly, Sean, *Elections,* Dublin, 1997 and 2002.

Flynn, *Oireachtas Companion*, Healy's, Dublin, 1923 to 1938.

Gallagher, Marsh, Sinnott, *How Ireland Voted*, Dublin, 1989 to 2002.

Magill Book of Irish Politics, Dublin, 1981.

Nealon Guides to the Dáil, Dublin, 1973 to 2002.

O'Leary, Cornelius, *Irish Elections 1918-1977*, G&M, Dublin, 1979.

Sinnott, Richard, *Irish Voters Decide*, Manchester University Press, 1995.

Walker, Brian (ed.), *Parliamentary Election Results in Ireland*, Vol 1, 1801-1922, RIA, Dublin, 1978. Vol 2, 1918-1992, RIA, Dublin, 1992.

General works:

Collins, Stephen, *The Cosgrave Legacy*, Blackwater, Dublin, 1996.

Coogan, Tim Pat, *De Valera: Long Fellow, Long Shadow*, Hutchinson, London, 1993.

Desmond, Barry, *Finally and in Conclusion*, New Island, Dublin, 2000.

Duignan, Sean, *One Spin on the Merry-Go-Round,* Blackwater, Dublin,1995.

Dwyer, Ryle, *De Valera: The Man and The Myths,* Mercier, Cork, 1991.

Farrell, Brian, *Chairman of Chief,* G&M, Dublin, 1971.

Fanning, Ronan, *Independent Ireland,* Helicon, Dublin, 1983.

Ferriter, Diarmuid, *The Transformation of Ireland: 1900-2000,* Profile, London, 2005.

FitzGerald, Garret, *All in a Life,* G&M, Dublin, 1991.

Foster, Roy, *Ireland 1600-1972,* Allen Lane, London, 1988.

Girvin, Brian, *The Emergency,* Macmillan, London, 2006.

Gaughan, J. Antrhony, *Thomas Johnson,* Kingdom Books, Dublin, 1980.

Horgan, John, *Seán Lemass,* G&M, Dublin, 1999.

Lee, Joe, *Ireland, 1912-1985,* Cambridge University Press, 1989.

Longford and O'Neill, *Eamon de Valera,* Arrow, London, 1970.

Lyons, FSL, *Ireland Since the Famine,* Weidenfeld & Nicholson, London, 1972.

Manning, Maurice, *Irish Political Parties,* G&M, Dublin, 1972.

Manning, Maurice, *James Dillon,* Wolfhound, Dublin, 1999.

McCullagh, David, *A Makeshift Majority,* IPA, Dublin, 1988.

McDonagh, Oliver, *The Emancipist: Daniel O'Connell,* 1989.

Ó Broin, Leon, *The Chief Secretary: Augustine Birrell in Ireland,* Archon, London, 1969.

Patterson, Henry, *Ireland Since 1939,* Oxford University Press, 2006.

Slivester, Christopher, *The Pimlico Companion to Parliament,* Pimloco, London, 1996.

INDEX

Churchill, Winston, 40, 44, 60, 100, 102, 114

Civil War, 66-7, 70, 72-7, 84, 90-1, 93, 105, 122, 137, 156-7, 183

Clann na Poblachta, 106-10, 116-18, 157

Clann na Talmhan, 101-2, 107-8, 110, 116-17, 120-21

Clarke, Kathleen, 66

Clarke, Tom, 66

Cluskey, Frank, 151, 165

Colley, George, 127-9, 131, 151-2, 169, 199

Collins, Michael, 56, 58, 60-5, 70-1, 73, 105, 138, 156-7, 193, 196

Connolly, James, 13, 103

Connolly, Patrick, 168

Cooney, Pat, 146

Cooper, Major Bryan, 81

Corish, Brendan, 124, 140-2, 149, 151, 165

Cosgrave, Liam, 86, 128, 134, 140-9, 151

Cosgrave, WT, 53, 56, 58, 60-2, 70-85, 88-94, 99, 108, 128, 157

Costello, Declan, 132, 154

Costello, John A., 109-12, 114, 116-18, 154

Cousins, Margaret, 42

Cowen, Brian, 213

Cox, Pat, 201

Craig, James, 38, 44, 59, 61, 98, 113

Cruise O'Brien, Conor, 132, 136, 138, 140, 142, 146, 155, 156, 169

Curran, John Philpot, 10

Currie, Austin, 185

D'Esterre, John, 16

Davitt, Michael, 12, 26, 51-2

De Rossa, Proinsias, 197

de Valera, Eamon, 9, 14, 49, 53, 56-8, 60-4, 70, 74-5, 79-81, 83, 85, 88-102, 105, 107-9, 111-12, 114, 116-20, 122, 126-30, 136-7, 141, 144, 157, 184, 204

de Valera, Síle, 152

de Valera, Vivion, 91

Democratic Left, 191, 195, 197, 202, 208, 212

Desmond, Barry, 136, 146, 173-4

Devlin, Joe, 113

Devoy, John, 51, 57

Dillon, James, 90-1, 99, 116, 124, 128, 131, 196

Dillon, John, 29

Disraeli, 26

Dockrell, Henry M., 85

Dockrell, Maurice E., 55, 85

Haughey, Charles, 9, 127-31,
133-5, 137-8, 150-3, 155,
158-65, 167-74, 176-82,
186-9, 198, 200, 204-6
Healy, Tim, 29
Hillery, Patrick, 127, 136, 149,
167, 184, 186
Hogan, Paddy, 77, 82
Home Rule, 25-9, 34-40, 43-8,
50, 59, 78, 113-14
Howlin, Brendan, 212
Hume, John, 189, 202
Hussey, Gemma, 184
Hyde, Douglas, 184
Independants, 59, 63, 65, 76,
81, 86, 90, 93, 97, 104, 108,
110, 116, 117, 125, 165-7,
176, 185, 201-2
Irish Parliamentary Party, 13,
26-30, 34-7, 44, 48-9, 51,
54-5, 59, 63, 68, 90, 113,
124, 196 see also Centre
Party
Jinks, John, 81, 82
Johnson, Tom, 76, 81, 104-5
Joyce, James, 30, 68
Keating, Justin, 132, 136
Kelly, John, 145
Kelly, Capt. James, 133
Kemmy, Jim, 166
Kennedy, Geraldine, 171, 168
Kennedy, Hugh, 78

Kenny, Enda, 206, 212-3
Keogh, William, 24
Kettle, Andrew, 67
Kettle, Tom, 67-6, 155
Kinnane, Patrick, 107
Larkin, Celia, 200
Larkin, Jim Jnr, 101, 104-5, 120
Larkin, Jim, 101-4, 107, 120
Larkin, Peter, 103
Lawlor, Liam, 205
Lefroy, Thomas, 21
Leigh, Mary, 41-2
Lemass, Sean, 80, 89, 122-9,
132, 137, 159, 197, 214
Lenihan, Brian, 127, 130, 177,
185-6
Lindsay, Patrick, 109
Loftus, Sean Dublin Bay, 166-7
Long, Walter, 59
Loughnane, Bill, 170
Lowry, Michael, 198
Lydon, Don, 179
Lynch, Jack, 127-5, 137, 140-1,
146, 150, 152, 160
Mac Bride, Sean, 106-9, 110-11,
115, 117-18
Mac Congháil, Muiris, 142
Mac Entee, Máire, 138
MacBride, John, 106
MacMorrough Kavanagh,
Arthur, 50

MacNeil, Eoin, 43, 47, 56, 69, 77

MacSharry, Ray, 160, 168, 171, 177, 188

Major, John, 189, 192-4

Mara, PJ, 208

Markievicz, Countess, 56, 66-7, 160

Martin Murphy, William, 85

Martin, Richard, 31

Mac Entee, Sean, 90, 117, 119, 137-8

McAleese, Mary, 186-7

McArthur, Malcolm, 168-70

McCarthy, Justin, 29

McCreevey, Charlie, 156, 169-70, 202, 208-9, 213

McDowell, Michael, 175, 210-11

McGilligan, Paddy, 82

McGrath, Joe, 79

McGuinness, Joe, 49

McKelvey, Joe, 73

McKenna, Joseph, 49

McQuaid, John Charles, 96

Meeham, Francis, 36

Mellows, Liam, 66, 73

Moore, George, 35

Morrissey, Dan, 111

Mulcahy, Richard, 77, 108-9, 124, 156-7

Mullen, Richard, 136

National Labour Party, 102-4, 108, 120

Noonan, Michael, 171, 206-7, 209, 212

Norton, William, 119-20, 124

Ó Caoláin, Caoimhghín, 211

Ó Dálaigh, Cearbhall, 148-9, 184

Ó Maille, Padraic, 73

O'Brien, Fergus, 187

O'Brien, William, 29, 36-7, 101, 103-4, 129

O'Connell, Daniel, 9-10, 12-23, 32, 55

O'Connell, Maurice, 32

O'Connell, TJ, 81, 105, 119

O'Connor, Frank, 37

O'Connor, Rory, 73, 89

O'Donoghue, Martin, 152, 160, 171

O'Duffy, Eoin, 91, 93-5

O'Faoláin, Seán, 37

O'Goman Mahony, James Patrick, 32-3

O'Higgins, Kevin, 77, 80

O'Higgins, Tom, 149, 184

O'Kelly, Seán 8, 89, 157, 184

O'Leary, Michael, 136, 165, 171

O'Malley, Dessie, 135, 152, 169, 174-5, 181, 188, 190, 200-1

O'Malley, Donogh, 127, 130